Will Smith

ACTOR

Black Americans of Achievement

LEGACY EDITION

Muhammad Ali	Martin Luther King Jr.
Maya Angelou	Spike Lee
Josephine Baker	Malcolm X
George Washington Carver	Bob Marley
Ray Charles	Thurgood Marshall
Johnnie Cochran	Barack Obama
Bill Cosby	Jesse Owens
Frederick Douglass	Rosa Parks
W.E.B. Du Bois	Colin Powell
Jamie Foxx	Condoleezza Rice
Aretha Franklin	Chris Rock
Marcus Garvey	Will Smith
Savion Glover	Clarence Thomas
Alex Haley	Sojourner Truth
Jimi Hendrix	Harriet Tubman
Gregory Hines	Nat Turner
Langston Hughes	Madam C.J. Walker
Jesse Jackson	Booker T. Washington
Magic Johnson	Oprah Winfrey
Scott Joplin	Stevie Wonder
Coretta Scott King	Tiger Woods

Will Smith

ACTOR

Anne M. Todd

CHELSEA HOUSE
PUBLISHERS
An imprint of Infobase Publishing

Will Smith

Copyright © 2010 by Infobase Publishing

Chelsea House
An imprint of Infobase Publishing
132 West 31st Street
New York, NY 10001

Library of Congress Cataloging-in-Publication Data

Todd, Anne M.
Will Smith : actor / by Anne M. Todd.
   p.   cm. — (Black Americans of achievement, legacy edition)
Includes bibliographical references and index.
ISBN 978-1-60413-713-2 (hardcover)
1. Smith, Will, 1968-   2. Actors—United States—Biography. 3. Rap musicians—United States—Biography. I. Title. II. Series.
PN2287.S612T63 2010
791.4302'8092—dc22   [B]   2010005689

Chelsea House books are available at special discounts when purchased in bulk quantities for businesses, associations, institutions, or sales promotions. Please call our Special Sales Department in New York at (212) 967-8800 or (800) 322-8755.

You can find Chelsea House on the World Wide Web at http://www.chelseahouse.com.

Text design by Keith Trego
Cover design by Keith Trego and Jooyoung An
Composition by Keith Trego
Cover printed by Bang Printing, Brainerd, MN
Book printed and bound by Bang Printing, Brainerd, MN
Date printed: July 2010
Printed in the United States of America

10 9 8 7 6 5 4 3 2 1

This book is printed on acid-free paper.

Contents

1

Standing Together

When Will Smith enters a room, he does so with a natural confidence, pride, and charm. From his 6'2" well-built frame and stylish apparel to his winning smile and approachable demeanor, Smith is the type of person who easily wins the hearts of those he meets. His ability to speak and to make direct eye contact with evident sincerity draws people to him—especially his most ardent fans, who come to see his movies in droves.

These likable, charismatic traits exuded from Smith on the night he stood on stage next to former heavyweight boxer Muhammad Ali at CBS Television City in Los Angeles, California, for a benefit airing live and commercial free on September 21, 2001. Smith and Ali were there to help raise money for United Way's effort to assist victims of the September 11 terrorist attacks and their relatives. While the shocked nation tried to understand and respond to the magnitude of the horrifying disaster, the charity show had been organized in just six days. So many celebrities wanted to contribute to the project that the potential playbill exceeded the show's time limits. Arrangements were quickly made for a celebrity phone bank to run simultaneously. To enable more celebrities to participate, some sat at long, narrow tables taking phone calls from the public and recording donations for the cause, while others made their way onstage. The cameras panned over to individuals in the phone bank throughout the event, including all the participants for the viewing audience.

As the show opened, the dark stage was dimly lit, illuminated only by hundreds of candles arranged behind the speakers, setting a quiet, somber tone. When Will Smith, dressed sharply in an all-cream suit with a white shirt, looked steadily into the camera and told television audiences across the world, "We are strongest when we stand together," it was evident that he meant what he said.

Numerous other speakers, singers, and entertainers graced the stage on this special tribute night. In addition to Smith and Ali, Julia Roberts, Tom Hanks, Cameron Diaz, Chris Rock, Lucy Liu, Tom Cruise, and George Clooney were just some of the many artists in attendance. Like Smith, speakers offered their condolences and words of encouragement. Hanks told the audience, "We are not heroes. We are merely artists and entertainers here to raise spirits and, we hope, a great deal of money."

Those performing musical numbers that evening included Alicia Keys, Billy Joel, the Dixie Chicks, Sheryl Crow, Paul Simon, and many others. Joel sang a version of his 1976 song "New York State of Mind." His performance was aired from a Manhattan studio via satellite for the show, and he noted that "there was a sense of inadequacy. I wish I could be down there moving wreckage and searching for bodies, but we can't, so this is what we do." About 89 million American viewers watched "America: A Tribute to Heroes." The stars helped to

Will Smith poses on the red carpet at the Vue Cinema on Leicester Square in London, England, on June 18, 2008, prior to the premiere of his film *Hancock*.

raise more than $200 million for United Way to assist the victims and their relatives.

When not helping to raise money for causes, Will Smith is busy starring in major Hollywood blockbuster films, writing and performing music, and running a production company. Smith might have a laid-back style—one in which he incorporates a bit of lightheartedness and fun—but this easygoing, self-assured guy is also intelligent and perceptive and has a drive that few could match. Smith told an interviewer, "I am one of the most obsessive people you will ever meet. I absolutely will not lose at anything. If you beat me, rest assured the best person in the world will be on a plane tomorrow to teach me how to do it better." Clearly, there is little stopping the dynamic, amiable Smith from achieving anything he sets his mind to.

Growing Up in West Philly

Of African-American and Native American heritage, Willard Christopher Smith Jr. was born in Pennsylvania to Willard Smith Sr. and Caroline Bright Smith on September 25, 1968. Will was the second of four children. Pamela, his older sister, had been born four years earlier. Will's younger siblings, Harry and Ellen, are twins, born in 1971.

Throughout his childhood, Smith listened to and learned from his parents. His mother, a graduate of Carnegie Mellon University, was a school administrator and worked for the School District of Philadelphia. She valued education and passed that value on to her children. Caroline made every effort to ensure that her children used correct grammar when they spoke and, when needed, she pointed out improper usage. She did not like hearing slang in her house. His mother's desire for him to study and work hard on schoolwork would lay the foundation on which Smith would build his future ongoing thirst for knowledge and desire to read up on any subject about which he might have a question. It is Smith's belief that even today he can find an answer to any question by reading a book.

Willard Sr. was a member of the U.S. Air Force until he opened his own refrigeration business. As owner and engineer in his new business, he installed the long freezer cases that are found in supermarkets. In addition, he ran an ice company that manufactured the large bags of ice that are sold to supermarkets. He valued a strong work ethic and passed this on to his children. Smith later described the extent of his father's devotion to getting the job done—no matter what—in an interview:

> I might have been about thirteen, and we went into the basement of a supermarket where he had to fix a compressor. A supermarket basement is just about the nastiest place in the world. . . . We go down there, our feet sticking to the floor, and I see this rat lying right where we need to be. This thing had eaten d-Con, which essentially burns its insides out and kills it. From the front it looked okay, but the rat's stomach and back legs were burned away. With his bare hand, my father tried to move it but it was stuck. So he yanked on it,

IN HIS OWN WORDS...

Will Smith learned much from his parents. One summer, his father told Smith and his brother that they were going to build a new brick wall in the family's refrigeration shop. Smith felt rather overwhelmed by the enormity of the project. And yet he kept uppermost in his mind the can-do attitude his father had passed down to him. As he later confided in an interview with *Reader's Digest*, Smith would tell himself, "I do not have to build a perfect wall today. I just have to lay a perfect brick. Just lay one brick, dude."

tore it loose and flipped it out of the way. Then he put his head down on the floor where the rat was, to do his work. Let me tell you, I never complained, from that day forward, about doing what I had to do to feed my family.

While Willard Sr. did not shy away from hard work, he also believed in the value of recognizing positive patterns or trends in life and applying the knowledge to use to his own benefit. For example, an observant child who notices that thriving stores are usually on busy streets will place his or her lemonade stand in the middle of the busiest park. In this way, Willard Sr. taught his children to keep their eyes open and be ready to take advantage of life's lessons and offerings in order to create a better life for themselves.

GROWING UP IN PHILLY

Busy, vibrant West Philadelphia, where Smith was born and raised, was home to people of many races and religions. West Philadelphia had large populations of Orthodox Jews, Baptists, and Muslims. The Smith family was Baptist. On Sundays, the family attended a Baptist church, where Will and his siblings took part in recitations and played the piano for the congregation. When Will would look out into the congregation and see his smiling grandmother with pride in her eyes he felt great. He also came to need that look of admiration—Will Smith wanted to make people proud. Yet he tried to keep his grandmother's sound advice in the forefront of his mind. She once told him, "Don't let failure go to your heart and don't let success go to your head."

Will had great respect for his grandmother. Her kind and big heart taught him the importance of acknowledging and respecting all people. Later in his life, he would talk to an interviewer about how some days he had come home from school to find his grandmother sitting in the living room chatting with homeless people she had met while out on errands.

Upon seeing Smith, she would inform him that she was going to let the people use the bath to wash up. These small acts of kindness had a big impact on Smith. He saw his grandmother as someone who believed she had a personal responsibility to help others. Echoing his grandmother's actions, he would grow up to become an active philanthropist.

Will and his siblings, despite being Baptist, attended a primarily white, Catholic school. But after school, Pamela, Will, Harry, and Ellen returned to their predominantly African-American neighborhood called Wynnefield, a middle-class area where the Smith family lived. Here, Will and his brother and sisters played mostly with black kids. He would later tell an interviewer from *Reader's Digest* that these socially inclusive experiences would help to shape his future comedy routines. He observed that the black community appreciated jokes about real life—wanting to laugh at hard times; the white community, on the other hand, appreciated jokes about fantasy—wanting to laugh about what could be. He found himself searching for jokes that would reach both communities. Because of this, he enjoys a diverse fan base today with no racial boundaries.

Like many kids growing up, Will encountered the occasional bully at school. Sometimes the bullies decided to settle things with their fists. In an interview later in his life, Smith recalled such a situation when a boy punched him square in the nose: "[The school bully] hit me right on the tip, the worst spot . . . makes your eyes water, you go flubberry for ages, all that. But for me, it lasted just two seconds. I was so amazed. I looked at this guy and he hit me again . . . and I thought, you're in so much trouble, because you can't hurt me." When Will realized this, his fear evaporated and bullies stopped picking on him. Years later, when making a film in which he played a boxer, he would use those emotions he felt as a child—first the fear of being hurt and then the realization that he could not be

(continues on page 12)

The enormously influential hip-hop group Grandmaster Flash and the Furious Five formed in the Bronx, New York, in 1978. Their groundbreaking use of break-beat deejaying, rapping, and turntablism pioneered hip-hop music and inspired young rappers like Will Smith. In 2007, they became the first rap group inducted into the Rock & Roll Hall of Fame.

Grandmaster Flash

Grandmaster Flash, as noted in *Rolling Stone*, is a pioneer in the development of two distinctive innovations in the music industry: the hip-hop sound and the "turntablist" DJ. Born Joseph Saddler on January 1, 1958, in Barbados, West Indies, he was raised in the Bronx, New York.

As a child, Saddler was fascinated by electronics and by his father's vast record collection. His mother, as he puts it, after watching him "hopelessly taking things apart to try to figure out how they worked" and messing around with "burned-out cars and her stereo," arranged for him to attend Samuel Gompers High School, a public vocational school. There, he studied math and science and acquired the technical skills to repair complex electronic equipment. He began spinning records on the Bronx street scene as a 15-year-old in 1973. While others excelled at break dancing, Saddler's passion for music and tinkering with sound equipment mushroomed. In an interview with PopMatters, he recalled:

> I tested the torque factor on different turntables. I had to figure needles out. See, there are two kinds, elliptical and conical. Ellipticals sound better, but they jump out of the groove really easily. Conical needles didn't sound anywhere near as good, but they stay in there without bouncing. As I was getting all the specs down, jury-rigging things and getting cursed out by people, I was also spending three or four years hanging out with the boys on the basketball court, with the girls at parties, finding out what people like.

Grandmaster Flash also intently studied the styles and techniques of popular DJs, especially Pete Jones, Kool Herc, and Grandmaster Flowers. Over time, experimenting with DJ gear and two turntables in his bedroom, he developed several groundbreaking DJ techniques. He describes the Quick Mix Theory as "a system for taking two records and manipulating them back and forth so that I could keep the instrumental break going for maybe 45 seconds, and then more." He explains that he developed the Clock Theory "to help me time records; you know, spin the record back two revolutions or whatever and then play the break, spin the other one back two, play, like that." His innovations with the turntable are considered standard DJ fare today.

He was also notorious for his technical tricks and maneuvers—mixing records under tables or behind his back and manipulating mixing faders with his feet. Very soon friends and fans dubbed him "Grandmaster Flash" because of his rapidly precise hand movements and overall dexterity with the turntables.

In the mid-1970s, Flash teamed up with rappers Kurtis Blow (Kurt Walker) and Lovebug Starski (Kevin Smith). He eventually began working with rappers Melle Mel (Melvin Glover), Cowboy (Keith Wiggins), Kid Creole (Nathaniel Glover), Mr. Ness a.k.a Scorpio (Eddie Morris), and Rahiem (Guy Williams). The sextet, known as Grandmaster Flash and the Furious Five, quickly became vogue throughout New York City.

In 1976, Flash and the Five debuted with a number of singles for the Enjoy label. All went largely unnoticed, though "Super Rappin'" had an underground following. Their 1980 release of "Freedom," with the Sugar Hill label, hit the top 20 on national R&B charts, moving toward selling more than 50,000 copies. But it was the revolutionary "The Adventures of Grandmaster Flash on the Wheels of Steel" that became the group's first milestone. That recording showcased Flash's cutting techniques, featuring a striking sound sequence created from clips of songs by Chic, Blondie, and Queen. "The Message," much darker and more keyed to urban issues than the group's previous party-style works, went platinum within a month of its release in 1982. "White Lines (Don't Do It)," an anti-cocaine single, followed in 1983.

Flash split from the Furious Five in the mid-1980s, recorded some music on his own, then faded from mainstream popularity. Well known as one of the founding fathers of hip-hop, he came back on the scene in the 1990s. Flash served as musical director and DJ of HBO's *The Chris Rock Show* in the late 1990s.

Grandmaster Flash won the BET "I Am Hip-Hop Icon" award in 2006. He was inducted, along with the Furious Five, into the Rock & Roll Hall of Fame in 2007—marking the first selection of a hip-hop group. In 2009, he was honored with the "Lifetime Achievement" award from the Urban Music Awards. DJ Hero, an Activision game released in 2009, featured his song "Boom Boom Tap" and Grandmaster Flash as a playable figure. Grandmaster Flash published his autobiography, *The Adventures of Grandmaster Flash: My Life, My Beats* in 2008 and released two new albums in 2008 and 2009. He also is owner of "G. Phyre," a line of clothing. It has been said that his "pioneering mixing skills transformed the turntable into a true 'instrument,'" and his "ability to get a crowd moving . . . made his DJ sets legendary."

(continued from page 8)

hurt—he could take care of himself. This kind of deep under-standing about himself helped Smith to build self-confidence and personal strength.

When Smith was 12 years old, he began rapping at parties with his friends. Rap is a popular kind of music that uses rhymes that are usually spoken or chanted instead of sung. A strong rhythmic accompaniment rounds out the sound. Rap first developed in African-American urban communities. Will had grown up idolizing comedian Eddie Murphy and rap legend Grandmaster Flash. Will did with his rhymes what many other rappers of the time did not—he wove comedy into the rap, giving his raps a distinctive feel. And although some rappers, including Public Enemy and NWA, began what is now called gangsta rap (which includes a considerable amount of cursing and allusions to violence), Smith stuck with a clean, wholesome sound with lyrics about the trials and tribulations of growing up. Smith's raps were not always so squeaky clean, however. In one interview, he recalls his grandmother coming across the notebook in which he wrote his first rap. When his grandmother saw that swear words appeared throughout, she did not tell him to take them out, but simply observed, "At least you happy with yourself." Thinking about this, he realized that the profanity did not make him happy and made a decision then and there to keep vulgarity out of his raps.

Young Will shared many beliefs and interests with his father—they both liked to look at the bigger picture, they both thrived under order and organization, they both loved chess (the father taught the son the game when the latter was about seven years old), and they both loved boxing. In particular, the older and younger Willard looked up to the great heavyweight boxer Muhammad Ali. Smith's father considered Ali a hero, though there were times that he disagreed with his choices—such as when Ali chose not to fight in the Vietnam War. Still, what drew both Will and his father to feel

Will Smith poses with students from his alma mater, Overbrook High School in Philadelphia, Pennsylvania, during MTV's *Total Request Live* at the MTV Times Square Studios in New York City, on March 29, 2005.

an appreciation and admiration for Ali was not whether he participated in wars; it was Ali's intense inner drive and his near-flawless boxing abilities.

But while Will enjoyed sports—both playing and watching them—his true love was music. He spent hours listening to rap and popular music and playing around with making his own. He could imagine himself onstage rapping and looking into the audience to find his loved ones watching him with the same pride he had seen in his grandmother's eyes when he was in church as a young boy.

When not rapping at parties or with his friends, Will tried to do his best in school. But he did not share his mother's passion for academics and found that he preferred spending time with his friends. Listening to comedy albums by Eddie Murphy and Richard Pryor was another favorite pastime. All of these activities were much more fun than doing homework. Still, Will was a bright student and even attended the prestigious Julia Reynolds Masterman Laboratory and Demonstration School—an academic magnet secondary school for select students of superior ability, located in the Spring Garden neighborhood of Philadelphia. Despite being very intelligent, he did not always live up to his abilities; he was an A student who turned in B work. Because he lacked the motivation and drive to live up to his potential in school, he frequently came home with lower grades than he should have.

CHANGES

Major change, however, was in store for the Smith family. When Will was 13, Willard and Caroline Smith separated and later divorced. Watching parents go through a separation is difficult for any child; luckily for Will and his siblings, his parents had consistently provided an incredibly loving and supportive home for their children. Still, he was not surprised by his parents' breakup, as they spent very little time together, had financial stresses on their shoulders regarding current bills and future schooling for the children, and were constantly dealing with the day-to-day issues that raising four children brings up. Facing all of these issues and problems, while at the same time feeling little support from the other spouse, doomed their relationship to failure. Caroline and the children moved out of the house and into her mother's house just a few blocks away. Because they were able to stay in the same neighborhood and keep the same friends, the move was not especially disruptive to the family.

Will faced another adjustment when he made the transition to high school. He attended Philadelphia's legendary Overbrook High School, a school that is well known for its famous alumni, including film producer James Lassiter, basketball stars Malik Rose and Wayne Hightower, sports radio icon Phillip Allen, astronaut Guion S. Bluford Jr., Negro League baseball legend Bill Cash, and Wilt Chamberlain, one of the greatest NBA players of all time. While at Overbrook, Will experienced the internal battle of conflicting goals: the ever-present pull from his mother to keep his focus on school, and a growing pull from his heart to create music. One thing was becoming clear—even more change was in store for Will Smith: Would he follow his mother's hopes for further formal education after high school? Or would he follow his heart?

3

The Fresh Prince

During his sophomore year at Overbrook High, Will Smith met Jeff Townes at a Philadelphia party. Townes had a following as a DJ at school and at block parties. Over the next couple of years, the two became good friends. Like Smith, Townes loved music and, at the early age of 10, had learned to scratch records—a popular trend in the 1980s, in which records were manually stopped and moved back and forth, producing a rhythmic scratching effect. When the two friends later decided to collaborate musically and write songs together at the start of Smith's senior year in high school, they became known as DJ Jazzy Jeff and the Fresh Prince. They created their own unique style—one that included scratching records, incorporating comedy, and profanity-free lyrics. Smith would later tell an interviewer, "I got broken in really early in the world of rap. There were always people who said my music was soft, that it wasn't real rap. My skin was toughened enough to laugh at that type of aspersion." Smith had the self-assurance to be proud of the music he was creating and to stand behind it.

DJ JAZZY JEFF AND THE FRESH PRINCE

Overall, high school was good for Smith. He did well academically and he was popular with both students and teachers alike. Smith had a poised, easy way with people and enjoyed making people laugh and making them comfortable. His charm and ability to talk himself out of trouble and onto people's good side earned him the nickname "Prince," given to him by his teachers at Overbrook. The nickname stuck. Soon, however, Smith learned that his charisma and popularity were not always enough to win someone over. When he was 16 years old, Smith's first girlfriend cheated on him. Smith would tell an interviewer of the incident, "In my mind, she cheated because I wasn't good enough. I remember making the decision that I will never not be good enough again."

At the start of his senior year of high school, Smith faced some important decisions. He had scored high on his SAT exam, and his mother had connections with the administration at the Massachusetts Institute of Technology (MIT) in Cambridge. Because MIT sought more black students, Smith would likely get in. Plus, there was a practical reason to attend the college: An education at MIT would almost certainly result in a substantial job, followed by financial security. Smith, however, had eyes for only one path: music.

Smith informed his parents that he would like to become a musician—more specifically, a rapper. His father could understand Smith's dreams, his mother less so. She had it in her head that Smith was going to go to school to become a computer analyst or a computer engineer. In the end, however, Smith's parents agreed to let Smith try rapping for one full year. If he were unsuccessful, Smith would let go of his musical ambitions and turn his attentions to college.

Not long before Smith and his parents' agreement, Smith and Townes met up again at a local party. Not only was Townes acting as DJ for the party, but also Townes's seasoned manager, James Lassiter, was in attendance and Smith had the chance to meet with him and talk. This time, Smith's personality and charm were enough: Lassiter was impressed. He saw potential in this personable and talented young man who could relate so

Hip-Hop

The cultural movement known as hip-hop, so prevalent in today's American mainstream, originated in the African-American communities of New York City in the 1970s. Since first emerging in the South Bronx, the popular lifestyle of hip-hop culture has spread worldwide.

The colloquial meaning of the word *hip* is "informed" or "current." Keith "Cowboy" Wiggins, who rapped with Grandmaster Flash and the Furious Five, coined the term *hip-hop* in 1978. Afrika Bambaataa, hip-hop trailblazer, DJ, and South Bronx community leader, defined the five essential components of hip-hop culture as "MCing, DJing, breaking, graffiti writing, and knowledge." Other elements include beatboxing, hip-hop fashion, and slang.

- MCing (a.k.a "rapping," "emceeing," "spitting bars," or just "rhyming"): An MC uses rhyming verses and wordplay usually delivered over a percussive rhythmic beat—sometimes prewritten, sometimes ad-libbed or freestyled—to introduce the DJ, to hype up the crowd, to promote him- or herself, and to comment on contemporary life and social issues. Often MC also refers to an artist with strong live performance skills. Melle Mel (Melvin Glover) of the Furious Five is one of the first rappers to call himself an "MC."

- DJing: A disc jockey (DJ or deejay) is a person who selects and plays recorded music for an audience. Hip-hop DJs use multiple turntables, often working with one or more MCs, and they often do turntable scratching to create percussive sounds. Kool DJ Herc, Grandmaster Flowers, Grandmaster Flash, Grand Wizard Theodore, and Grandmaster Caz were DJs well to his audience. Smith and Townes wasted no time. They started meeting in order to write and rehearse new raps. Soon, they performed in Battle of the Bands at the 1986 New Music Seminar. Jeff took first place in the DJ competition. The attention they received at the New Music Seminar was enough to help them get noticed by the music industry. DJ Jazzy Jeff and the Fresh Prince signed a recording contract with Jive Records.

who extended the boundaries and techniques of normal DJing for the hip-hop culture.

- **Breaking (a.k.a "b-boying" or "break dancing"):** Breaking is a dynamic, energetic, acrobatic style of dancing, developed as a part of hip-hop culture by African-American and Latino youths in New York City. The accompanying music features prolonged musical breaks created by the DJ remixing the music. The dancer is called a b-boy, b-girl, or breaker—with the "b" standing for "beat." B-boys intentionally add quick stops and falls to their routines to add a sense of spontaneity.

- **Graffiti writing:** Graffiti—writings or drawings scribbled, scratched, or sprayed illicitly on a wall or other surface in a public place—came into being in the late 1960s, primarily used by political activists. In the early 1970s, graffiti writing exploded throughout the New York City subway system, where writers added their street number to their nickname—for example, TAKI 183 and Tracy 168. Bubble lettering from the Bronx dominated at first, but Brooklyn's more complex "wildstyle" became the standard. Hip-hop graffiti is known as a visual expression of rap music.

- **Beatboxing:** Beatboxing is a form of vocal percussion of hip-hop culture. Using the human mouth, lips, tongue, and voice, the artist produces drumbeats, rhythm, and musical sounds. It may simultaneously involve singing, the imitation of turntablism, and the simulation of other musical instruments.

In 1987, before Smith had even graduated from high school, the two friends released their debut album, *Rock the House.* The 10 raps included on the album were "Don't Even Try It," "Girls Ain't Nothing but Trouble," "Guys Ain't Nothing but Trouble," "Just One of Those Days," "Just Rockin'," "The Magnificent Jazzy Jeff," "Rock the House," "Special Announcement," "Takin' It to the Top," and "Touch of Jazz." In their collaborations, Smith produced most of the rhymes, while Townes master-minded the mixing and scratching.

DJ Jazzy Jeff and the Fresh Prince's debut single, "Girls Ain't Nothing but Trouble," from the debut album, was developed from a segment of the theme song from the 1960s television sitcom *I Dream of Jeannie.* The success of both the single and *Rock the House* made Smith a millionaire. He was only 18 years old. His financial success was short-lived, however, when—after foolishly spending a large portion on expensive houses and cars and gifts for his family and friends—he had to give nearly all the money he had left to the IRS. Later he would confide to an interviewer, "I had a hit single on the radio for 30 days before I graduated from high school. And that's dangerous. You don't want to have a hit record on the radio when you're in high school."

Despite Smith's poor money management during this early opportunity, he was able to learn from the experience and ensure it did not happen again. And he would soon be in a position to test what he learned, as it would not be long before the young rising star would make a lot more money. Smith and Townes spent almost all their free time working on new music and trying out new rhythms and raps.

In 1988, DJ Jazzy Jeff and the Fresh Prince released their follow-up album, *He's the DJ, I'm the Rapper,* which included the radio hits "Parents Just Don't Understand," "Brand New Funk," and "Nightmare on My Street." In 1989, Will Smith and Jeff Townes won the first-ever Grammy to be given to a rap artist for the album *He's the DJ, I'm the Rapper.* It became

From left, DJ Jazzy Jeff (Jeff Townes) and the Fresh Prince (Will Smith) are seen backstage at the American Music Awards ceremony in Los Angeles, California, on January 31, 1989, shortly after winning in the categories of Favorite Rap Artist and Favorite Rap Album.

the first hip-hop album to ever go double platinum. Also, in 1989, DJ Jazzy Jeff and the Fresh Prince made another hit record, *And In This Corner* . . . Although this third album hit gold, it failed to do as well as their previous two albums.

Caroline Smith would later tell an interviewer how she came to realize her son was on his way to stardom. "My daughter and I were walking down 52nd Street one day and in the window [of a store] is *He's the DJ, I'm the Rapper*." Caroline knew then that there was no way her son was going to become a computer analyst or a computer engineer. Smith had definitely proved to

his parents—and to himself—that music was an industry in which he could flourish and become successful.

THE FRESH PRINCE OF BEL-AIR

Around this time, Benny Medina, a producer, talent manager, and record executive, was developing an idea for a sitcom that he pitched to NBC. The plot centered on a young kid from Philadelphia who was sent to live with his wealthy relatives in Bel-Air, California. When choosing a male lead to play the starring role, NBC had to look no further than the charismatic, new-to-the-scene young rapper (who just happened to be from Philadelphia) they had seen in music videos. Will Smith, despite having no real training as an actor, was cast in the lead role of the street-smart Philadelphia kid. The experience of having done some music videos for his albums gave Smith some know-how about being in front of a camera. And the role fit him perfectly—so much so that NBC named the show *The Fresh Prince of Bel-Air*, using Smith's rapper name in the title.

Cast in the roles of the relatives in Bel-Air were James Avery (who played the father, Philip Banks), Janet Hubert (who played the mother, Vivian Banks), Karyn Parsons (the older daughter, Hilary), Alfonso Ribeiro (the son, Carlton), Tatyana Ali (the younger daughter, Ashley), and Joseph Marcell (the family butler, Geoffrey). Occasionally, Townes

DID YOU KNOW?

Jada Pinkett, who later became Will Smith's wife in real life, tried out for the role of his character's girlfriend on *The Fresh Prince of Bel-Air*. Nia Long was cast in the part instead when executives at NBC decided Jada was too short. Actress/dancer Debbie Allen directed the show's pilot, which aired on September 10, 1990.

Will Smith performs during the taping of his successful television sitcom series, *The Fresh Prince of Bel-Air*. Smith played the title role for six seasons, from 1990 to 1996.

made recurring guest appearances on the show as Smith's best friend, "Jazz." In the first season, the two friends never failed to greet each other with their signature handshake— swinging "mid-five, point-back/snap" with both characters saying "Pssh!"

Although Smith had had some experience in front of the camera and did have natural acting ability, he nevertheless prepared for his TV role, just as he has done with all of his undertakings. He learned not only his own lines, but memorized all the lines of every character. (He would later joke about how you can see his lips moving as he mouths every actor's lines in the early episodes of the show.) In addition to making sure he was entirely prepared for his role, Smith studied the other actors and tried to learn from the way they delivered lines, the way they moved, and the way they interacted in front of the camera. He used his time on the set of *The Fresh Prince of Bel-Air* to polish and perfect his delivery. His hard work paid off. The successful show lasted for six seasons, from 1990 to 1996. During that time, Smith had made a name for himself in Hollywood as an up-and-coming sitcom star.

In addition to working on the long-running show, DJ Jazzy Jeff and the Fresh Prince continued to make music. In 1991, they released *Homebase*, with the singles "Summertime" and "Ring My Bell." Smith and Townes would later win a Grammy Award for "Summertime," which was about the summers growing up in Philadelphia. People of all ages could relate to and appreciate the song. Smith told an interviewer for *JET*: "There's no experience I've ever had that beats standing in the middle of a stage with 70,000 people and those first couple of seconds of 'Summertime' come on. That feeling is—well, there's nothing like that." In 1993, the duo released their final album together, *Code Red*, with the hit "Boom! Shake the Room." While *Code Red* did not do as well as the previous albums, "Boom! Shake the Room" became a number-one hit in the United Kingdom.

Following *Code Red*, Smith decided to take a break from music. He had been juggling the demands of taping his sitcom and recording music for years. It was time to stop working in

Will Smith's Albums

DJ JAZZY JEFF AND THE FRESH PRINCE

1987 *Rock the House*
Includes the tracks: "Girls Ain't Nothing but Trouble" and "Rock the House"

1988 *He's the DJ, I'm the Rapper*
Includes the tracks: "Nightmare on My Street," "Parents Just Don't Understand," and "He's the DJ, I'm the Rapper"

1989 *And in This Corner . . .*
Includes the tracks: "I Think I Can Beat Mike Tyson" and "Too Damn Hype"

1991 *Homebase*
Includes the tracks: "I'm All That," "Summertime," and "You Saw My Blinker"

1993 *Code Red*
Includes the track "Boom! Shake the Room"

SOLO ALBUMS

1997 *Big Willie Style*
Includes the tracks: "Gettin' Jiggy Wit It," "Just the Two of Us," "Big Willie Style," and "Men in Black"

1999 *Willennium*
Includes the tracks: "Will 2k," "So Fresh," and "Wild Wild West"

2002 *Born to Reign*
Includes the tracks: "Act Like You Know," "Block Party," and "I Gotta Go Home"

2005 *Lost and Found*
Includes the tracks: "Switch," "Tell Me Why," and "Loretta"

two time-consuming arenas. Though Townes and Smith are still close friends and still perform and record occasionally, at this point Smith decided to narrow his focus and turn all his energies to acting. Following the unofficial breakup of DJ Jazzy Jeff and the Fresh Prince, Townes went on to become a prominent R&B, soul, and neo-soul record producer. He also founded the A Touch of Jazz Productions company in his hometown of Philadelphia.

GETTING STARTED IN THE MOVIES

Smith's Hollywood adrenaline was pumping, and he was ready for new projects. He had made a name for himself in music. He had made a name for himself in television. Now he wanted to make a name for himself in movies. It was not all smooth-sailing, however, trying to break into the movie industry. His manager, James Lassiter, would later tell an interviewer of Smith's struggle to break into the field, "Nobody cared. You're [just] a rapper. You got lucky, and you do this television show, but that's all you can do." Smith and Lassiter did not give up. Lassiter continued to look for parts for his client, and Smith continued to do auditions for small movie roles in order to get his foot in the door.

He got his chance in 1992. In this year, while still working on *The Fresh Prince of Bel-Air*, Smith took on his first movie role. He had a small part in *Where the Day Takes You*, a film directed by Marc Rocco, about a group of homeless runaway teenagers who are trying to survive on the streets of Los Angeles. Film critic Roger Ebert said of the film, "The movie is effective, well-acted, and convincing." Also in 1992, Smith married Sheree Zampino and had a child, Willard III, who was called Trey. Smith and Zampino were young, however, and their relationship could not withstand the challenges of one partner having such an all-consuming career path. The marriage only lasted three years.

A year later, in 1993, Smith took another small part in a film called *Made in America*, directed by Richard Benjamin.

The movie starred Whoopi Goldberg and Ted Danson. Smith played the wisecracking best friend of Goldberg's daughter. Roger Ebert said this film "isn't a great movie, but it sure is a nice one." The *Washington Post* noted of Smith's performance, "Smith's shtick and probably his character are superfluous, but Benjamin sensibly indulges the young comic. Considering the maudlin mood swing that's in store, the audience is going to need all the laughs it can get."

Also in 1993, Smith landed a role in the film adaptation of the hit play *Six Degrees of Separation*, directed by an Australian named Fred Schepisi. Starring in the film with Smith were Stockard Channing and Donald Sutherland. John Guare had authored the play and the screenplay. The story is about a hustler (Smith's character) who cons his way into the Manhattan apartment of a wealthy couple (Channing's and Sutherland's characters) by convincing them he is the son of noted actor Sidney Poitier and their son's friend from school. Schepisi brought his own cinematographer, Ian Baker, to work alongside him in the film.

Onstage, Guare had been working with a set of three actors who he believed fit the leading roles perfectly. He worried about recasting the part of Paul, the hustler. Then someone suggested to him that Will Smith, the bright, young actor

IN HIS OWN WORDS...

Will Smith grew up loving movies. When he was about eight or nine years old, he saw the movie *Star Wars* for the first time and later told an interviewer:

[*Star Wars*] was the movie that put me into a space where the science fiction element was almost a spiritual connection for me. I thought, if someone could imagine that and then put it on a screen and make me feel like that. . . . And my entire career I've been trying to make people feel like *Stars Wars* made me feel.

from the popular sitcom *The Fresh Prince of Bel-Air,* try out for the role. Guare had reservations. For six months he would not meet Smith. Finally, he gave in and appeared on the set of *Fresh Prince.* Smith later recalled to an interviewer:

> [Guare] walked into my dressing room, saw I had a picture of Run DMC next to one of Mao, and he said, "Oh my God, you're him, you're Paul!" I never read a piece of dialogue. [Guare] said, "You get it!" He hugged me, said he was so excited because he never thought there was a chance it would work.

Convincing the film's director, Schepisi, however, that Smith was the man to play Paul took a bit more persuasion. Schepisi would tell an interviewer:

> Everybody got excited about Will, but I was a little more cautious. I interviewed a lot of actors. But Will tried to convince me that he'd do whatever it would take, would go through whatever process, was sure he could get himself prepared. The confidence and charm was everything the character should be. [He was] worth taking a chance on.

With the role under contract, Smith got to work. Even before rehearsals began, he trained three times a week for three months with both a dialect coach and an acting coach. Once rehearsing and filming began, Schepisi realized Smith was perfect for the role of Paul. But then the day rolled around Smith was to film an on-screen kiss with Anthony Michael Hall, the prep-school student infatuated with Paul. Smith told Schepisi he would not do it. In the end, Schepisi had to use a double and show only the backs of their heads. Smith would later admit that "it was very immature on my part. I was thinking, 'How are my friends in Philly going to think about this?' I wasn't emotionally stable enough to artistically commit to that aspect of the film." Smith realized once the filming was done that he had made a mistake. He knew that he should have given a full commitment to the part. It was a valuable lesson for him.

Still, Smith proved to critics across the country that he was more than just a sitcom actor—he had natural talent and skills. *Variety* noted, "Smith proves himself an extremely charismatic presence, convincing in his sincerity and cunning in conveying his ability as a human sponge." Other reviewers called Smith's acting "enigmatic," seductive," and "complex." Despite good reviews, *Six Degrees of Separation* made very little money.

It was the summer of 1995 when director Michael Bay's *Bad Boys* hit theaters. This high-budget cop movie starred Smith (as Detective Mike Lowery) and Martin Lawrence (as Detective Marcus Burnett)—two black actors from a background of sitcoms—Smith from *The Fresh Prince of Bel-Air* and Lawrence from *Martin*. Critics did not give the movie high reviews, though many reviewers praised Smith's and Lawrence's acting abilities. *Rolling Stone* said:

> [Smith and Lawrence] are primed to explode. And they do, though the script doesn't do them any favors. It's a familiar mix of jolts and jokes. But the bad boys achieve something a budget can't buy: an easy, natural rapport that makes you root for them. For comedy and thrills, Lawrence and Smith are a dream team.

In fact, the MTV Movie Awards nominated them for the Best On-Screen Duo award. It would be the first of many accolades Will Smith would earn for his acting abilities.

4

Box-office Superstar

As his father had taught him, Will Smith knew he had to keep his eyes open and figure out life's opportunities for himself. Smith had arrived in Hollywood with manager James Lassiter and a plan. Smith had wanted to become a star. He had wanted to become the biggest name in movies. While Smith tested the waters in small parts, he and Lassiter carefully studied the wider, overall picture. Smith later told *Reader's Digest* that he and Lassiter noticed

> that of the top ten movies of all time, ten were special effects or animation. Nine were special effects or animation with creatures. Eight were special effects or animation with creatures and a love story. So we made *Independence Day*. When you see the patterns, you just try to put yourself in the position to get lucky.

Smith got lucky—very lucky—though with some excellent strategy, thanks to his father.

INDEPENDENCE DAY

As Smith had predicted, *Independence Day* proved to be a huge summer blockbuster. Directed by Roland Emmerich (who also wrote the screenplay, along with Dean Devlin) and released in 1996, the film drew big box-office numbers. In the movie, Bill Pullman plays President Thomas J. Whitmore and Jeff Goldblum plays David Levinson, a tech-whiz who helps to stop aliens from destroying the Earth. Smith's character, a U.S. Marine Corps pilot named Captain Steve Hiller leads a counterattack against the invading aliens. When one alien proves difficult to deal with, Smith's character then immediately punches the slimy alien and asks, "Who's the man, huh?"

Smith's experience working with Emmerich was a good one. Emmerich allowed the actors room to explore and improvise. Devlin noted that over half the dialogue in the scenes that Jeff Goldblum shared with Judd Hirsch and Will Smith was improvised.

Smith would tell one interviewer when she asked when was the last time someone called him Fresh Prince, "It was

IN HIS OWN WORDS...

Will Smith does not believe in backing down. He does not believe in giving less than he is capable. His success comes from pushing himself to be more than he thought possible. In one of Smith's songs he writes, "The key to life is on a treadmill. I'll just watch and learn while your chest burns. Because if you say you are going to run three miles and you only run two, I don't ever have to worry about losing something to you." Similarly, he told an interviewer at *Reader's Digest*, "When I say I am going to run three miles, I run five. With that mentality, it is actually difficult to lose."

**Shown from left are Will Smith (as Captain Steven Hiller), Ross Bagley
(as Dylan Dubrow), and Vivica A. Fox (as Jasmine Dubrow) in a scene
from *Independence Day* (1996), Smith's first box-office smash hit.**

the Monday after *Independence Day* opened and all the 'Hey,
hey, Fresh Prince! Fresh Prince!' stopped. When the box-office
numbers came out after *Independence Day*, it was suddenly
[in a deep voice]: 'Good morning, Mr. Smith.'" Smith had
now shown the world that he was a full-fledged actor to be
taken seriously—one who could fill theaters and sell tickets
like few others.

Despite the movie's box-office draw (the opening weekend
in the United States brought the film more than $50 million),
not all film critics enjoyed the film. A critic for Reelviews said,
"*Independence Day* turns out to be overlong, overblown, and

overdone." Roger Ebert had mixed feelings about the film, noting, "*Independence Day* is in the tradition of silly summer fun, and on that level I kind of liked it, as, indeed, I kind of like any movie with the courage to use the line, 'It's the end of the world as we know it.'"

MEN IN BLACK

In 1997, big changes were afoot in Smith's life. For starters, he married once again. This time, it was to actress/singer Jada Pinkett, whom he had met some years earlier. They are still married today and have two children, Jaden and Willow. Trey Smith, Will's son with his former wife, lives with them as well. That same year, *Men in Black* opened in theaters—another enormous hit for Smith. In this movie, Smith, as NYPD officer James Darrel Edwards III (a.k.a Agent J), was once again fighting aliens and saving Earth. Barry Sonnenfeld directed this blockbuster film; Ed Solomon wrote the screenplay. Starring with Smith was Tommy Lee Jones, as secret Agent K, a veteran MIB agent who is partnered with Smith. Agent J and Agent K try to save the world when they learn that aliens have threatened to blow it up. Smith described the differences between *Men in Black* and *Independence Day* to an interviewer:

> They're two very different kinds of movies—*Independence Day* was more of a good old-fashioned disaster movie, and this one has more of a comic edge. And we didn't think we were making another summer blockbuster, until Barry [Sonnenfeld] started spending all that money, then it had to be!

Most audiences and critics enjoyed the movie. Movie reviewer James Berardinelli said *Men in Black* "is a snappy, clever, often-funny motion picture that provides the perfect blend of science fiction-style action with comic dialogue." A reviewer for *Rolling Stone* wrote, "Director Barry Sonnenfeld loads the bases with action, fantasy, and laughs, and hits a grand slam—there's no need to ask the question ['Who's the man?,' as Smith had in *Independence Day*]: Will Smith is indisputably the man." The *San Francisco Chronicle* enjoyed Smith's performance, but thought the rest of the film lacked substance and laughs. The newspaper's reviewer wrote, "Good thing for Sonnenfeld and producer Steven Spielberg that they landed Will Smith as one of those bureaucrats. Jones, cold, sardonic and world-weary, is all too convincing as a government agent. Smith is unimaginable in the role, but that's to his credit. His ease, his warmth and comic timing graft a good nature on the film that can't legitimately be inferred from the material."

Smith wrote two songs for the movie. He told an interviewer, "I'd been away from music for about four years, but I did the two songs on the *Men in Black* soundtrack, and then I signed a new deal with Columbia Records. The record company has some smart people working there, and it feels good to have the opportunity to make some real records." The album, which would include the theme song, "Men in Black," was Smith's first solo record, *Big Willie Style*. Another hit song on *Big Willie Style* was "Just the Two of Us." This song is about being a dedicated father to Trey. *Big Willie Style* went on to become multiplatinum. Smith, excited to be back in the music scene, said, "Rap's gone through a sort of dark ages. With the loss of Biggie and Tupac, the industry is ready for a change. I'm just feeling good to be a part of the renaissance." The hit single "Gettin' Jiggy Wit It" earned Smith the first No. 1 single of his solo career. The success of *Independence Day* and *Men in Black*—both with their huge U.S. opening weekend sales (*Independence Day* made over $50 million and *Men in Black* made over $84 million)—led Smith to term his weekend-opening blockbusters as a "Big Willie Weekend."

BRANCHING OUT

In addition to making films, Smith teamed up with his brother, Harry, to establish Treyball Real Estate in the late 1990s. Harry worked to develop and execute projects that included hotel, spa, and residential deals. Harry later shifted the company's focus to only residential development, renaming it Treyball Development. Its Web site maintains, "By accepting nothing less than the best in quality, working with the most elite brands, and providing access to otherwise inaccessible events, opportunities, and products, Treyball aspires to be the leader in Luxury Lifestyle Living."

Also around this time, Smith and his manager Lassiter started their own production company, Overbrook Entertainment. The company produces plays (*Jitney*); films (*Ali, Showtime, Saving Face, Hitch, ATL, The Pursuit of Happyness, I Am Legend, Hancock, Lakeview Terrace, The Secret Life of Bees, Seven Pounds,* and *I, Robot*); television (*All of Us*); and music (*The Evolution of Robin Thicke, Wicked Wisdom*). Originally, Overbrook dealt with Universal Pictures to produce movies, but three years later when nothing materialized, they switched to Sony. In recent years, the company has also profited by exploring the foreign market and producing films in other countries, as they have now done in Russia (promoting *I, Robot*), South Africa (promoting *Ali*), and India. As Lassiter noted about a recent deal with India, "We don't want to plaster Mumbai with pictures of Will Smith. We want to make an exchange. We want to do films there as well as introduce Indian actors and directors to the United States. We have to show people we are willing to adapt to their world."

Enemy of the State, which opened in theaters in 1998, was Smith's next acting project and costarred Gene Hackman. David Marconi wrote the screenplay, and Tony Scott directed the film. Smith was eager to work with Hackman, an actor he admires. *Rolling Stone* called the movie a "dynamite thriller." *Enemy of the State* earned Will Smith an NAACP Image Award nomination for Outstanding Actor in a Motion Picture. *Rolling Stone* would write, "[Producer Jerry] Bruckheimer and director Tony Scott have wisely set their course by Will Smith, who is sensational in a dramatic role that leans on him to carry a movie without the help of aliens or Big Willie-style jokes for every occasion." Film reviewer James Berardinelli agreed:

> Smith's work in *Enemy of the State*, which requires him to portray the proverbial ordinary guy caught up in extraordinary circumstances, may be the most accomplished of his career. He succeeds in making audiences believe that [his character] Robert Dean is just like us, not an over-the-top clown or macho superhero with bulging biceps. We identify with him.

And Smith continued to draw crowds. In its opening weekend in the United States, *Enemy of the State* made more than $20 million.

It was on the set of *Enemy of the State* where Smith ran into a bit of competition in a game he loved: chess. As previously mentioned, he had been playing chess since he was seven years old, back when his father taught and coached him. Smith and his dad had played many games together and Smith rarely loses a game. Yet on the set of *Enemy of the State*, an older gentleman beat Smith at chess. Of the experience, Smith told an interviewer, "The next day I found a chess master to train me for the next three months so I could beat that dude before the movie was over." True to form, before filming ended, Smith had beaten the gentleman at chess.

The following year, in 1999, Smith made a poor choice that led to regrets later. First, he turned down the lead part of Neo in *The Matrix*, a science-fiction film that would go on to earn rave reviews. Instead, Smith met his first major movie flop, when he appeared in a sci-fi cowboy western film called *Wild Wild West*. Smith had been looking forward to taking part in a film based on one of his favorite childhood television programs, *The Wild Wild West*, which first ran from 1965 to 1969. Once again, Smith was teaming up with director Barry Sonnenfeld. Also starring in *Wild Wild West* was comedian Kevin Kline. While the film was unsuccessful despite its opening-day numbers, Smith's musical track from the film was a hit—a song that could be found on his 1999 album, *Willennium*. Smith would later tell an interviewer, "My biggest emotional defeat and the greatest emotional pain I've had as an actor was when *Wild Wild West* opened up to $52 million. The movie wasn't good. And it hurt so bad to be the number 1 movie, to open at $52 million and to know the movie wasn't good."

Reviewers had little good to say about the film. Roger Ebert called it "a comedy dead zone." James Berardinelli wrote "[*Wild Wild West*] lacks energy and the characters display little charisma." The *San Francisco Chronicle* noted that Sonnenfeld "can't seem to get anything going here." Overall, critics seemed to agree that *Wild Wild West* was simply a bad film.

Released the following year, in 2000, *The Legend of Bagger Vance* helped Smith to regain his momentum. The movie is based on a novel by Steven Pressfield (Jeremy Leven wrote the screenplay) in which a struggling golfer attempts to recover both his game and his life with help from his mystical caddy. Smith's character, Bagger Vance, was the golf caddy to Matt Damon's struggling golfer, Rannulph Junuh. The characters' names, "Bagger Vance" and "R. Junuh" are representations of Bhagavan (Krishna) and Arjuna, taken from the Hindu text, *The Bhagavad Gita*. What lessons Damon's character (Junuh) learns during the movie are based loosely on those Krishna teaches to Arjuna while pretending to be his humble chariot driver.

The film, directed by Robert Redford, received somewhat mixed reviews from audiences and critics. On the one hand,

Ebert wrote, "Will Smith could make Bagger Vance insufferable, but the part is written and played to make it more of a bemused commentary. He has theories about golf, and ways of handling his player, and advice, but it is all oblique and understated. No violins." Berardinelli, on the other hand, called the movie "pretentious."

In 2001, Smith released a children's book based on his 1997 song "Just the Two of Us." Published by Scholastic Books, the text of the 32-page book, also called *Just the Two of Us*, is composed of Smith's lyrics illustrated with Kadir Nelson's emotional drawings. *Publishers Weekly* said of the book:

> Describing the night he brought his newborn son home from the hospital, Smith states, "That night I don't think one wink I slept/ As I slipped out of my bed, to your crib I crept/ Touched your head gently, I felt my heart melt/ 'Cause I knew I loved you/ more than life itself." Emotion also runs deep in the paintings, which show the boy growing into a youth. The pictures rely on fairly conventional imagery: father holding up infant son against the sun, the two viewed in profile; father and mature son in thoughtful conversation on a beach at sunset. But Nelson effectively conveys the affirming message of the text.

Smith could now add published author to his growing list of noteworthy accomplishments.

9/11

On September 11, 2001, terrorists from the al-Qaeda network, under orders from Osama bin Laden, destroyed the World Trade Center in New York City and severely damaged the Pentagon outside of Washington, D.C. After hijacking four commercial U.S. airplanes, the terrorists crashed the first plane into the north tower of the World Trade Center and a second plane into the south tower. A third plane hit the

Pentagon, and the fourth plane went down in a Pennsylvania field after some of the passengers were successful in thwarting the hijackers. The people aboard all four planes were killed instantly. Almost 3,000 people died in the attacks and scores more suffered health problems related to the attacks. Additionally, businesses crumbled. People lost their jobs and their homes. The cost to clean up the attack was estimated at approximately $600 million. The events of 9/11 would affect the lives of the American people for years to come.

People across the United States and around the world were stunned and horrified by the terrorist attacks. Like many other people, famous and obscure, Will Smith wanted to help. Along with hundreds of other celebrities, he took part in a televised telethon that helped to raise money for United Way's effort to assist the victims and their relatives. Called *A Tribute to Heroes*, the program helped to raise more than $200 million for the cause.

ALI

Meanwhile, Michael Mann, director of such notable films as *Heat* (1995) and *The Insider* (1999) was working hard to bring to the screen a movie called *Ali* about the legendary heavyweight boxer Muhammad Ali. This film, which appeared in theaters in December 2001, brought Smith back to the peak of his game.

Smith was to star as Muhammad Ali, someone who Smith had followed and admired since childhood. This seemed to be a role perfect for Smith. Or was it? Mann had already approached him to play the part six years earlier. Smith had turned him down. He would tell an interviewer, "I was 27 and not ready emotionally or physically. I was looking at Denzel Washington and Larry Fishburne and I just didn't feel I possessed that level of artistry." Now, six years later, he again sat across from Michael Mann to discuss the film. Perceptively sensing Smith's psychological turmoil, Mann told him:

I know you're scared and you're right. You mess this up and it's all over. It's a very bad idea to be making this movie. Everyone in the world has an opinion about Muhammad Ali and you're too famous. This is really a role for an unknown . . . you're absolutely at the wrong point in your career to be doing it. And that's exactly why you should do it. We're not going to do what people have seen; we're going to find the Muhammad Ali who lived between the well known moments.

Muhammad Ali

One of the greatest heavyweight boxers of all time, Muhammad Ali (originally Cassius Marcellus Clay Jr.) was born in Louisville, Kentucky, on January 17, 1942. Ali's feats in the ring are recognized worldwide. In the 1960 Olympic Games in Rome, Ali fought as an amateur in the light heavyweight division for the United States—he brought home gold. Later, in his career as a professional, he became the first three-time world heavyweight champion.

Young Cassius's eyes and heart were first opened to boxing as a 12-year-old. In 1954, he and a friend were attending an annual convention of the Louisville Service Club, which featured a black merchant bazaar at the Columbia Auditorium. Leaving after free popcorn and ice cream, the friends discovered that their bicycles had been stolen. Cassius was told to report the theft to a policeman who would be at the boxing gym in the basement of the auditorium.

Fuming that his new red-and-white Schwinn bike had been stolen, Clay poured out his story to the white policeman, named Joe Martin, who was also boxing coach at the Columbia Gym. When Cassius declared he wanted to "whup" the thief, Martin asked if he knew how to fight. The worked-up boy answered, "No, but I'd fight anyway." Martin advised the preteen to hang around the gym and learn something about fighting before making any more "hasty challenges." Soon Martin became Clay's first trainer, working with him through his explosive six-year amateur career.

Clay also worked with Fred Stoner, an African-American trainer at the local community center. Stoner honed Clay's talents to win six Kentucky Golden Gloves titles, two national Golden Gloves titles, an Amateur Athletic Union national title, and the light heavyweight gold medal in the 1960 Summer Olympics. Nicknamed "The Greatest," "The Champ," and "The Louisville Lip,"

Mann's speech clicked, producing a responsive chord in Smith. So even though Smith continued to hear from people why he should *not* do the film, that he would live to regret it, he did not listen to them. Despite the fear of the enormity of the task he was about to tackle, deep down, he believed he was born to play the role. Smith later told an interviewer, "There are roles you are born to play. Muhammad Ali just happened to be the guy I could relate to spiritually and emotionally, down to his attraction to women."

Clay amassed an amateur record of 100 wins, 5 losses. Clay's professional career began back in Louisville after the Olympics. His first professional fight, in 1960, was a win in a six-round decision over Tunney Hunsaker.

Now fighting as a heavyweight, Clay had an unusual style. The norm for that weight division meant defending the face by carrying the hands high. Instead, Clay carried his hands low and perfected and depended on quickness and foot speed to avoid punches.

In 1964, after joining the Nation of Islam, Clay changed his name to Muhammad Ali. Opposing the Vietnam War because of his religious beliefs, Ali refused to be inducted into the U.S. military in 1967. The harsh consequences included arrest and being found guilty of draft evasion as well as being stripped of his heavyweight boxing title. Though not imprisoned, his boxing license was suspended, forcing him to abandon boxing for four years. His appeal, which worked its way up to the U.S. Supreme Court during those four years, was honored. Ali returned to professional boxing and tallied a record of 61 total fights, 56 wins, 37 wins by knockout, 5 losses, 0 draws, and 0 no contests. After defeating every top heavyweight in his era (dubbed the golden age of heavyweight boxing), he retired from boxing in 1981.

In 1984, Ali was diagnosed with Parkinson's syndrome, a neurological disease to which boxers are more susceptible due to severe head trauma. Despite the disability, he remains active in public service. In 1985, he was the guest referee at the inaugural WrestleMania event. In November 2002, serving as U.N. Messenger of Peace, he went to Kabul, Afghanistan, for a three-day goodwill mission. In Louisville, in 2005, he founded the nonprofit Muhammad Ali Center, which promotes peace, social responsibility, personal growth, and respect.

From left, Michael Bent and Will Smith in a scene from *Ali*, in which Bent portrayed boxer Sonny Liston and Smith portrayed boxer Muhammad Ali. In order to transform himself into the former heavyweight champion, Smith had to put on considerable muscle mass and learn how to box.

In order to make the film as authentic as possible, Mann worked extensively with Smith for nearly two years prior to the release of the film. Smith trained hard; former boxer and trainer Darrell Foster (who once trained Sugar Ray Leonard) worked with the actor to teach him to fight. Smith would later tell an interviewer, "For the initial 14 months, [Foster's] approach was not to teach me to fight like Ali. [Foster] taught me to fight, feeling that once I knew how to fight, as an actor, I'd learn how to fight like Ali." Learning to fight meant training six months with headgear and six months without. Halfway through the intense training, Smith was nearly ready to quit but decided against it. He realized, as he told an interviewer:

> I had the rest of the year to go! When you get to that point, it makes other things seem less difficult. For example, I could ask my wife to pick up the kids . . . but if I work fourteen hours and *still* pick up my son, that makes me a better father. And [the kids] may not understand it now, but in years to come, it'll register.

After much of the training was complete, Muhammad Ali himself came to watch Smith fight in the ring. Smith recalled Ali's reaction to an interviewer, "When [Ali] came down the first time, he was really excited. It was great to watch his eyes, because even at his age, he is still amazed by himself. He is looking at me, but he is really looking at himself. He told me I got him so excited that he was going to make a comeback."

Mann helped the actors get into their roles by insisting that shoots go on location in Africa (where Ali knocked out George Foreman in a pivotal match) rather than simulate somewhere in Mexico or in the Caribbean. In traveling to Africa, the actors could fully experience what the real-life people had felt and experienced, thus bringing more heart to their acting. Smith and his wife, Jada Pinkett, bought a house in Africa to live in during their stay. Of his time there, Smith said, "The experience in Africa was amazing. I had dinner with Nelson Mandela. . . . Africa is the best and the worst of everything that exists on this planet, the most beautiful land you will ever see in your life."

Mann and Smith had to juggle their desire to be authentic with the limitations of a two-hour movie and the difficulties of portraying a living figure. They decided that Smith would try to capture an interpretation of Ali, rather than just impersonate him. Not all movie critics felt this was the way to go, however. Roger Ebert wrote of the film, "Smith is the right actor for Ali, but this is the wrong movie. Smith is sharp, fast, funny, like the Ali of trash-talking fame, but the movie doesn't unleash that side of him, or his character." Other critics appreciated Smith's acting abilities. *Variety* noted, "Smith . . . carries the picture with consummate skill." And movie reviewer Berardinelli wrote:

> Little blame for *Ali*'s weaknesses can be laid at the feet of actor Will Smith, who, like Denzel Washington in *Malcolm X*, put his whole heart and mind into the performance. The actor bears only a passing physical resemblance to Ali, but, as with Anthony Hopkins in Oliver Stone's *Nixon*, Smith proves that great acting can overcome the need to look like a twin. This portrayal is at times passionate and fiery, and at others, quiet and thoughtful. Smith's Ali is a portrait of a man who was a fighter both inside and out of the ring. His work here will force those who doubted his selection to eat their words.

All of Mann's and Smith's hard work had ultimately paid off: Smith was nominated for an Oscar for best actor at the Academy Awards. The one-time Fresh Prince was not only a huge box-office draw, but was now also regarded as a serious actor.

5

Continuing Movie Success

Will Smith had proved himself a multifaceted dramatic actor to be taken seriously. His role as Muhammad Ali showed his dedication and skill as an actor. Following *Ali*, Smith unfortunately made a couple of uninspired sequels—*Men in Black II* (2002) and *Bad Boys II* (2003). *Men in Black II*, again directed by Barry Sonnenfeld and costarring Tommy Lee Jones, proved to be too close a repeat of the first movie. Film critic Roger Ebert pointed out, "This is a movie that fans of the original might enjoy in a diluted sort of way, but there is no need for it—except, of course, to take another haul at the box office." Ebert also noted that "Smith and Jones fit comfortably in their roles and do what they can, but the movie doesn't give them much to work with."

Similarly, *Bad Boys II*, directed—like the first *Bad Boys*—by Michael Bay and costarring Martin Lawrence, met with poor reviews. Of this movie sequel, Ebert wrote, "*Bad Boys II* is a bloated, unpleasant assembly-line extrusion in which there are a lot of chases and a lot of killings and explosions." Although the movies were not box-office failures, they were not nearly as successful as the originals.

ALL OF US

Smith and his wife cocreated and produced a television sitcom for UPN, *All of Us*, which premiered in 2003. The show, about a blended family (with biological and stepparents) similar to the Smiths', starred Duane Martin and Lisa Raye. The Smiths' son, Jaden, had a recurring role as Reggie. *USA Today* wrote, "Despite an overall feeling of goodwill, 'All of Us' has a tendency to push too hard in the wrong spots. . . . Still, though it may not be doing so convincingly, 'All of Us' is addressing a common modern family situation, and that's not a bad place for a situation comedy to start."

After the sitcom's third season, UPN merged with The WB to form The CW network. The new network picked up *All of Us*, which got the sought-after time slot behind the hit series *Everybody Hates Chris*. During its four-year run, *All of Us* was nominated for an NAACP Image Award in the Outstanding Comedy Series category in 2007.

I, ROBOT

In 2004, Smith starred as Detective Del Spooner in the adaptation of Isaac Asimov's sci-fi classic, *I, Robot*, directed by Alex Proyas. Smith told Blackfilm.com that

> the great thing with Alex is that his strong point will be the things that people [in the audience] are going to love, but that studios are going to be dying [from], . . . he wants to make art films. He's committed to the artistry of the film period. . . . Alex pushes the envelope everywhere, just to take six minutes for that interrogation scene, just the pace, it's

an art film pace, it's not action, summer blockbuster pace, and I think that's what makes him special, and whatever he wants to make I will make it with him.

Proyas thinks just as highly of Smith. Proyas told *USA Today*, "[Smith is] one of the last true leading men. There's a connection he has with audiences who will see him in anything he does. I don't quite know how you explain that kind of magic."

Smith's character is a police officer investigating a murder in the year 2035. The film also stars Chi McBride, Bridget Moynahan, Bruce Greenwood, James Cromwell, and Alan Tudyk. Smith told *JET*, "What attracted me to this film is the concept that the robots aren't the problem. The technology is not the problem. It's the limits of human logic that are the problem, and essentially we are our own worst enemy." He also said that he was attracted to the blend of genres *I, Robot* contains. It is not only an action film but also a mystery. Smith found that combination intriguing, as action movies are generally fast paced, while mysteries are generally slower paced. Plus, as he told Blackfilm.com, "I just loved the idea, the gamble of making this kind of movie, because it's actually a small art film that is masquerading as a big summer blockbuster."

The visual effects in *I, Robot* allowed the robots (which in reality were computer-generated images) to appear as if they were interacting with the humans. As Smith noted to interviewer Paul Fischer:

> The process was somewhat easier because technology has grown to the point where now they can actually use a person. So they had the guys in green suits, which meant being able to play the scene with a person [and it] actually gives a real organic texture to it versus looking at a [stand-in] tennis ball.

The special effects team included John Nelson, Andy Jones, Erik Nash, and Joe Letteri. The film was an Oscar nominee for Best Achievement in Visual Effects at the Academy Awards in 2005. The film pulled in top dollar at the box office, with an opening weekend of more than $52 million.

The visual effects and Smith's captivating performance wowed critics and fans alike. One reviewer said of his acting in *I, Robot*:

> Without support from Martin Lawrence, Tommy Lee Jones, Gene Hackman, Jeff Goldblum, or Kevin Kline, [Will Smith] shows that he's got enough charisma and energy to hold a viewer's attention. Plus, he can deliver the mandatory one-liners with as much brio as [Arnold] Schwarzenegger or [Bruce] Willis. Despite the physicality of the role, Smith manages to connect with the audience in everyman fashion, and, although the part requires a certain amount of wit, he doesn't play it like a clown.

Although Smith may have let down some fans with the sequels he made of *Men in Black* and *Bad Boys*, *I, Robot* surely restored any doubt in his fans' minds that he was still firing on all cylinders.

SHARK TALE AND HITCH

In 2004, Smith took on his first animation film when he gave voice to Oscar (a fish) in the children's movie, *Shark Tale*. Providing voices to the characters along with Smith were Robert De Niro, Renée Zellweger, Jack Black, and Angelina Jolie. Film critics were not especially impressed with the DreamWorks production, though in its opening weekend in the United States, the movie earned more than $47 million. Smith proudly brought his entire family to the New York City premiere of *Shark Tale*, happy that he was able to share one of his films with his youngest children, Jaden and Willow.

The following year, disaster struck the southern United States when, on August 28, 2005, Hurricane Katrina hit just north of Miami, Florida. Four days later, the eye of the hurricane hit Louisiana early in the morning. A few hours later, much of the levee system in New Orleans collapsed, causing Lake Ponchartrain and the Mississippi River to flood nearly all of New Orleans. The hurricane damaged coastal regions of not only Louisiana, but also the neighboring states of Mississippi and Alabama. More than 1,000 people died because of the hurricane, which also caused about $200 billion in damage and displaced over one million people. Thousands of displaced people were bused to neighboring states.

One of the heroes of the tragedy was John Keller, a resident of New Orleans. John "The Can Man" Keller received his nickname because he rescued 244 of his neighbors from the five-story American Can Company apartment complex in Mid-City. Eleven feet of water had trapped the residents inside the apartment building. The Can Man worked for five days, fighting off looters and searching for victims trapped inside, bringing them to the rooftop for safety when he found them. When a rescue operation was finally put into place, the Can Man oversaw the process from the building's rooftop. Will Smith, along with his production company Overbrook Entertainment, and Sony, bought the rights to John Keller's story. John Lee Hancock is going to write and direct the movie (currently titled *The American Can*) and Smith will star as Keller and coproduce the film. As of 2010, the film is still in development.

Branching out yet again, Smith tried his hand at a romantic comedy in 2005, with his role as Alex Hitchens in *Hitch*. (In addition to acting in *Hitch*, Smith once again wrote and performed the theme song. He would include it on his album, *Lost and Found*, also released in 2005.) Andy Tennant directed the film, and Kevin Bisch wrote the screenplay. Eva Mendes and Kevin James also starred in the film. James described working with Smith to an interviewer:

Will Smith holds a framed Guinness World Records certificate as he arrives for the premiere of the film *Hitch* at Leicester Square in London, England, on February 22, 2005. That day, Smith broke the world record for the most public appearances by a film star in 12 hours by attending three different premieres in Manchester, Birmingham, and London.

> Working with [Smith] is a lot like [working with] Martin
> Lawrence—they just wear their hearts on their sleeves, you
> just see it—it's all right there, there's nothing hidden and
> it's a really powerful comedic tool when people can just see
> through you in that way and I'm predicting that [Smith's]
> going to be a really huge movie star. He's a genius.

Hitch, making history as the first romantic comedy to star minority actors in the lead roles, received favorable reviews from critics. The *Los Angeles Times* said, "Smith is a gifted comic actor, and seeing him in a lighthearted comedy, his first romantic lead, is a pure pleasure." When *Hitch* premiered in Europe, Smith earned himself a spot in the Guinness Book of World Records when he made the most public appearances in 12 hours on February 22, 2005. On this day, he walked the red carpet three times in England to introduce the premieres of *Hitch* at Manchester, at Birmingham, and then in London. (Smith would lose this title in October 2006 when German actors Jürgen Vogel and Daniel Brühl attended four red-carpet premieres for their movie, *Ein Freund von mir.*)

THE PURSUIT OF HAPPYNESS

When Smith was offered the opportunity to work on the film *The Pursuit of Happyness* (2006), he jumped at the chance. The film, directed by Gabriele Muccino, is based on the life of a man named Chris Gardner, who in the early 1980s, was a single father living on the streets of San Francisco, California. Gardner believed he could make something of his stymied life and did everything he could do to turn his life around. He had managed to secure a job as a medical equipment salesman, but he did not make enough money to afford housing. Living on the streets with his young son, he cleaned up in public bathrooms and went about trying to sell his equipment.

One day, Gardner saw a man getting into a fancy red Ferrari. Gardner asked the man what he did for a living, and the man responded that he was a stockbroker. Gardner very quickly decided he too would become a stockbroker. Taking an interest in the bright, eager Gardner, the stockbroker, named Bob Bridges, met with him a few times to talk about the financial industry. Bridges even made arrangements for Gardner to meet with branch managers at major stock brokerage firms. In this way, Gardner ended up in a training program with E.F. Hutton and then eventually in another training program at Dean Witter Reynolds. Even while working at the firm for a year, none of his coworkers realized that Gardner and his son were homeless.

After years of hard work and refusing to give up, Gardner managed to save enough money to open his own brokerage firm and eventually became a millionaire. Even at the lowest times, he did not lose hope—he held onto a faith and a determination in himself—qualities that Will Smith greatly admires. Smith notes in one interview:

> Chris Gardner laid down in a bathroom with his only child, seemingly the ultimate parental failure. The next morning, he woke up, he bathed his son in the sink and he went to work. You can't do that if there's a possibility this might not work out. You can't do that. You have got to believe that it's already a done deal. It's just a matter of time before you get what you're designing.

Smith connected with Gardner's desire to win and make something of himself because he too was one to make a plan, to have an idea about something, and to follow through until the end to ensure it happened.

Smith brought the script home and began to study it. Smith's younger son, Jaden, was listening to his father read the script aloud. After Smith had finished reading, Jaden told his father he wanted to play the role of the son. Smith helped to arrange for an audition for Jaden so that his son could fulfill

Jaden Smith and Will Smith film a scene for *The Pursuit of Happyness*, a 2006 film directed by Gabriele Muccino, in which Smith portrays a real-life salesman who attempts to take care of his son while living on the streets and struggling to become a stockbroker.

Chris Gardner

Christopher Paul Gardner was born in Milwaukee, Wisconsin, on February 9, 1954. His roller-coaster life personifies the rags-to-riches model in dramatic fashion. From a chaotic childhood, his own broken marriage, fathering a son with a girlfriend, low-paying jobs, and a desperate yearlong period of homelessness on the streets of San Francisco, he skyrocketed to self-made success—becoming a millionaire entrepreneur, motivational speaker, author, producer, and philanthropist. Gardner's memoir, *The Pursuit of Happyness*, was published in May 2006.

As a child, Gardner lacked positive male role models. His absent biological father, Thomas Turner, was living in Louisiana, and his stepfather was physically abusive. Gardner and his three half sisters lived in constant fear of the raging man. The children were placed in the foster care system twice by the time Gardner was eight years old.

Although his mother, Bettye Jean Gardner, was imprisoned more than once due to her volatile marriage, Gardner acknowledges her "spiritual genetics" as one source of his determination to survive and his eventual stunning achievements. Bettye Jean inspired strength, self-pride, and self-reliance in him. He quotes her as saying, "You can only depend on yourself. The cavalry isn't coming." Gardner's early exposure to alcoholism, domestic and child abuse, illiteracy, extreme fear, and powerlessness planted the seeds for his fighting against them in the future.

Gardner also credits the love and high expectations of his two children, Christopher Jr. and Jacintha, for his steady climb from dysfunctional family to self-made wealth and success. Chris Jr. was a toddler and Jacintha not yet born during Gardner's homeless period, when he was scrambling for shelter on the streets. In a slight departure from Gardner's life story, the motion picture *The Pursuit of Happyness* (2006) depicts Gardner's son as a five-year-old.

Using ingenuity, resourcefulness, and perseverance, Gardner managed to rise above his destitute circumstances. By 1987, with start-up capital of just $10,000, he launched a brokerage firm, Gardner Rich & Co., from his Presidential Towers apartment in Chicago, Illinois. In 2006, after selling Gardner Rich in a multimillion-dollar deal, Gardner became CEO and founder of Christopher Gardner International Holdings, which has offices in Chicago, New York, and San Francisco. As a philanthropist, Gardner funds many charitable organizations, most notably the Cara Program, now located in Chicago, and the Glide Memorial United Methodist Church in San Francisco, which had sheltered father and son when they were homeless.

his dream but did little else. He explained to an interviewer, "I was in [Jaden's] corner, but I didn't have his back. He earned the job himself, and that's the way it's supposed to be." Jaden was not the only young boy who wanted the role—about 100 other boys auditioned for the part. Producer Jason Blumenthal described the difference between Jaden and the other candidates: "Then we met Jaden Smith and it was night and day. Jaden was this kid. He came in with sincerity, honesty, and rawness. We cast the absolute best person for the job."

Working with Jaden on the film proved a fulfilling experience for both of them. Jaden even helped his father work through difficult scenes. Smith would confide to an interviewer, "I was struggling with a scene. Seven, eight times [Gabriele Muccino] was coming up and giving me notes." Smith described how Jaden leaned over to whisper to him that he was doing the same thing on every take. He then thought about what Jaden had said and realized his son had something there. In another interview, Smith described what he had learned from Jaden's comment, "I started watching him and he's doing what acting is really supposed to be—he's living in the moment. He's pure and natural in the moment. That's what actors look for. That's the nirvana, where you're natural and living in the moment." Watching his son work was eye-opening for Smith:

> [Jaden is] so natural and I've reevaluated how I perform and I stopped preparing. That is the way that I have adjusted my acting style. I went back and got coaches to help me strip away all the "thinking" I've done up to this point, the mechanical. I've got good "moves" and he helped me create new "moves." With this movie, the new moves are no moves.

The Pursuit of Happyness received mixed reviews, but all agreed that the acting by the two Smiths was outstanding. A reviewer for Variety.com noted, "The younger Smith is allowed to deliver a natural, childlike performance" and the elder Smith "throws his all into the role." *Rolling Stone* said, "Smith wins our hearts without losing his dignity, as Chris suits up for success by day and fights off despair by night. The role needs gravity, smarts, charm, humor and a soul that's not synthetic. Smith brings it. He's the real deal." A critic for the *Los Angeles Times* declared that *The Pursuit of Happyness* was an "unexceptional film with exceptional performances." Indeed, Smith was again nominated for an Academy Award for best actor for that exceptional performance.

6

Life Off-screen

Although advancing his music and acting career are both top priorities in his life, family life has always been highly important to Will Smith. As mentioned previously, Smith has been married twice and has three children. On May 9, 1992, Smith married fashion design student Sheree Zampino. Smith had met Zampino at a taping of the television sitcom *A Different World* back in 1991. The couple had one son, Willard III (also known as Trey), born in November 1992, before divorcing in 1995. Smith feels badly about the breakup, believing that he could have fixed their problems but that he gave up on the relationship before it had a chance to mature.

Then on December 31, 1997, Smith married Jada Pinkett; they are still married today. The two walked arm in arm down the aisle at their lavish wedding, giving each other away in front of about 100 friends and relatives who had come to witness the event. The gesture of giving each other away was a symbol to represent the equality of their relationship. The wedding took place at Cloisters, a medieval-style mansion near Pinkett's hometown of Baltimore, Maryland. Smith and Pinkett wore clothes designed by Badgley Mischka; Pinkett carried a stunning arrangement of pink and white flowers. The bride and groom read letters they had written to each other at the ceremony professing their love. Once the letters were read, Pastor Marvis May of Baltimore's Macedonia Baptist Church pronounced Will Smith and Jada Pinkett Smith husband and wife.

Smith believes the key to the success of their marriage is communication. They also have a deep understanding and respect for one another. Smith describes to *Rolling Stone*:

> There's a lot going on in my mind, things I want in life, so being my friend and, even more so, being my wife is not to be entered into casually. I demand attention because I'm never complacent. With me it will never be "This is where we're going." It's "This is where we are now, but we're going somewhere else." Most women would say, "Can't we stay here a minute?" But I have a sense there's always something greater.

When explaining their mutual understanding of their respective roles in the marriage, Jada said in an interview with

IN HIS OWN WORDS...

Perhaps rooted in the generous character of his grandmother, Will Smith feels he has much to offer the world. He told *Rolling Stone*:

> Right now, I make people laugh. It's an important service to make people feel good. But I want to be here for a bigger reason. And I measure my greatness—or lack thereof—in the number of people I move, help, or make life better for.

Will Smith, his wife, the actress Jada Pinkett Smith, and their family arrive to the premiere of *Hancock* at Grauman's Chinese Theatre on June 30, 2008, in Hollywood, California. Family is a central focus of Smith's life.

Child Magazine, "He's the dynamic energy of this family and I am the internal magnetic energy. That's what makes it all work." She continues, "One thing I *have* learned is that women really can have it all. When I first had a family, I believed that I had to be a stay-at-home mom. I've gone through many transitions to figure out what I can/can't be—and as of right now, I can be a lot of things."

Jada believes the two of them connect on many levels. She says of her husband, "He's smart yet gritty, streetwise and creative. Will's one of those people who can take you to a Tupac concert one night and the next to an opera. And that's who I am. It's hard to find somebody to connect with you on all those levels." But Smith and Pinkett did find each other, and every day their relationship and bond seem to grow stronger.

Along with Smith's son from his first marriage, Will and Jada had two children together, Jaden (born July 1998) and Willow (born Halloween 2000). When asked in an interview if the couple wanted more children, Jada responded, "No, my plate is very full. . . . There are my children in my family and in my community who need our love and assistance and attention." In speaking about her hopes for their children's future, Jada said, "I just want to have happy kids who live with a sense of integrity. I have no control over what they decide to do or who they decide to marry. All I can do is help create a foundation so that they can know how to find happiness." The Smith family of five loves and supports one another unconditionally.

JUST FOR FUN

In his spare time, Smith runs to keep healthy and fit. He views running as a way to face your own worst enemy—that voice in your head that tells you to run only three miles instead of five because your ankles hurt. It is the same voice, Smith believes, that will tell your 16-year-old self that you are not cool unless you smoke a joint or will tell your 30-year-old self that your wife will not find out if you have an affair. Smith uses running as a way to practice his beliefs in setting goals, ignoring the voice that tells you to slack off, and to achieve what you set out to do.

Music remains, just as it was when he was child, one of Smith's greatest passions. With his success in the movies, he can afford to make any kind of music he chooses. He told an interviewer, "I create the music that's in my heart. I talk about the things I feel, and I am in a position that a lot of guys aren't in. I don't have to rap for money. I make what I want the way I want to make it. It's hard for me to outwardly condemn people for trying to feed their families." Will performed at the Live 8 concert in Philadelphia alongside his former partner, DJ Jazzy Jeff, in July 2005.

Smith is a kid at heart. In an interview, he said, "Fresh Prince reflects pretty much the core of my personality. The level of goofiness I exude in that show matches the level I exude daily with my kids and my family. I am very silly." When time allows, Smith plays chess and video games with his kids. Smith seeks out all kinds of high-tech toys; he loves finding the newest gadgets and latest technology. He told *JET*, "I'm a real science-fiction junky, so the concept of future technology is always interesting to me. I've got all the latest everything." Such a passion for cutting-edge technology is also seen in his business decisions. The Boom Boom Room—developed and owned by Smith and located in Burbank, California, just blocks from several major entertainment studios—features state-of-the-art sonics along with the latest recording gear and technology. Providing the "most comfortable and secure facility in the Greater Los Angeles area," clients can relax while enjoying a top-notch, worry-free recording experience.

Smith is also a big reader. He believes he can find answers to any problem—old or new—by reading the proper book.

Nearly every year, Smith takes his mother, Caroline, to the Canyon Ranch spa in Tucson, Arizona, for a vacation. Although Caroline now wears a prosthetic leg after breaking her left leg and then needing amputation after a bad infection, she spends much of her time helping others. She volunteers at the Maternity Care Coalition, located right in the same neighborhood where she raised Will Smith and her

Jada Pinkett Smith

On September 18, 1971, in Baltimore, Maryland, Adrienne Banfield gave birth to a baby girl and named her Jada Koren Pinkett. The baby girl's ancestry was West Indian, Creole, and Portuguese Jewish. Banfield, who was pregnant with Jada while in high school, later married the father, Robsol Pinkett Jr., a contractor; the marriage lasted only a few months.

Much of Jada's childhood was spent in the rundown Pimlico section of northwest Baltimore. At the age of 14, however, she won a place at the Baltimore School for the Arts, where she majored in dance and choreography, graduating in 1989. One of her classmates there was rapper Tupac Shakur. A top-selling recording artist, he was also a budding actor and a social activist. Jada remained close friends with him until his death following a drive-by shooting in Las Vegas, Nevada, in September 1996.

Jada moved to Los Angeles after studying theater for a year at the North Carolina School of the Arts. She began acting in 1990 with a part in *True Colors*, a short-lived sitcom. Her career started to blossom with a role in the long-running NBC series *A Different World*, produced by Bill Cosby. Overall, she has appeared in more than 20 films, the most widely acclaimed being *Ali*, *The Matrix Reloaded*, and *The Matrix Revolutions*.

Trying her hand at business ventures, Jada opened her own music company, 100% Womon Productions and, in 1994, created Maja, a line of clothing featuring women's T-shirts and dresses bearing the slogan "Sister Power." The fashions are sold mostly in small catalogs.

Jada met actor Will Smith when she auditioned on the set of Smith's television show *The Fresh Prince of Bel-Air*. The two married in 1997 and she adopted the name Pinkett Smith. They have two children, Jaden and Willow. Pinkett Smith is also stepmother to Trey, Smith's son from a previous marriage. Although they have homes in Philadelphia, on Star Island in Miami other children. She notes that "there are probably a lot of things I could do, but it probably wouldn't be as fulfilling as working with the babies."

Because Will and Jada believe in a hands-on approach to parenting, they take their roles as father and mother very seriously. Instead of sending their kids to public schools, they have decided to homeschool their two younger children,

Beach, Florida, and in Stockholm, Sweden, their primary home is a 27,000-square-foot mansion on 100 acres in the mountains near Malibu, California.

In 2002, under the stage name Jada Koren, Pinkett Smith formed the highly successful metal rock band Wicked Wisdom, for which she is lead vocalist and songwriter. "I listened to all kinds of metal as a kid. Metallica, Guns N' Roses. I would always look at Axl Rose and say, 'Why aren't there any chicks out there doing this now?' I always wanted an opportunity to get out there and rock out." Pinkett Smith also directs music videos for newly emerging rap groups.

Pinkett Smith published her first children's book in 2005. Featuring Pinkett Smith and her daughter, Willow, the book is titled *Girls Hold Up This World*. When asked what message she hoped to convey in her book, Pinkett Smith replied, "Don't be afraid to be you. Know that you are exceptional. You can do anything if you believe in it and are motivated to work for it. That's a message I feel that young girls often don't get. We spend a lot of time trying to live up to someone else's ideas of who we should be." In 2005, along with many other celebrities, Pinkett Smith invested in Carol's Daughter, a line of beauty products for African Americans, created by Lisa Price. Pinkett Smith serves as spokeswoman for Carol's Daughter.

Pinkett Smith regularly pays motivational visits to shelters and inner-city schools. Additional humanitarian work is directed to children and families suffering in South Africa. Citing her "superb artistic work in film and music and her humanitarian efforts in youth education and family welfare both nationally and internationally," Harvard College Dean Benedict Gross named Pinkett Smith the Harvard Foundation's 2005 Artist of the Year.

"I'm a lot of things," Pinkett Smith says. "We all are as women. And if I'm not allowed to be all those things, I lose that vibrancy and that light that makes me beautiful."

while Trey, the eldest, attends a private high school. Smith believes that memorizing obscure facts and figures is not what an education should be about. He would rather his children read, for example, Plato's *Republic* and Aristotle's *Politics*. So the Smiths hire teachers and experts to come in and work with their children on specific assignments such as these, as well as tutors to teach the basics—reading, writing, and arithmetic.

The Smith kids are not always busy being homeschooled or making movies. Sometimes they simply like to hang out with their friends. Pinkett Smith told *Child Magazine*, "All those kids also have their friends over, so we usually have at least eight children running around playing basketball or video games. Last weekend, we had a boys' night and took all the boys with us to screen one of Will's new movies. Our house is always active."

While parenting and homeschooling take a lot of time and energy, the couple makes time for each other. The Smiths have a solid, stable relationship. To achieve this, they stay in touch no matter where their acting careers may take them and take time to talk when they are together. They try to set aside Sundays to be family days—maybe going on a picnic or to a museum. In one interview, Pinkett Smith recalled one Sunday when it was just herself and Smith: "It doesn't take a lot of time ... it's just about being aware and present enough to know what the other person wants. What does *he* want today?" In addition, Smith and Pinkett Smith are comfortable about not agreeing on everything. They respect each other, and they respect what they create together in their relationship. Pinkett Smith told an interviewer:

> We hardly ever agree on anything, and we've learned to really respect that in our relationship. You might have an idea in your mind of what a marriage is supposed to be, and you're driving, driving, driving toward this ideal picture.

But you have to be open to the fact that your relationship is meant to be something else.

POLITICS AND RELIGION

Like many in Hollywood, Will Smith is a politically liberal Democrat and does not shy away from taking a political stand. In January 1993, he hosted the Presidential Inaugural Celebration for Youth as part of the gala for President Bill Clinton. In 2008, Smith supported Senator Barack Obama of Illinois with donations to his presidential campaign on the Democratic ticket. When Obama was elected president of the United States, Smith was deeply moved. He wrote:

> For me, it was something that I've always believed. I've read the Declaration of Independence. I've read the Constitution. I have the preamble memorized. It's something I've always believed in, and when Barack Obama won, it validated a piece of me that I wasn't allowed to say out loud—that America is not a racist nation.... I don't think we are African Americans, Irish Americans, or Japanese Americans anymore. I think Americans are a new race of people. We are Americans of African decent. We are Americans of Irish decent. It's a whole new world.

More recently, accompanied by their two younger children, Jaden and Willow, Smith and Pinkett Smith hosted the Nobel Peace Prize Concert at Oslo Spektrum in Oslo, Norway, on December 11, 2009, which honored the 2009 Nobel Peace Prize winner, President Obama.

Smith's views on religion are open-minded, inquisitive, and, in the end, personal. He once explained to an interviewer:

> I'm a student of world religion, so to me, it's hugely important to have knowledge and to understand what people are doing. What are all the big ideas? What are

people talking about? I believe that my connection, to my higher power, is separate from everybody's. I don't believe that the Muslims have all the answers. I don't believe the Christians have all the answers, or the Jews have all the answers, so I love my God, my higher power. It's mine and mine alone. I create my connection and I decide how my connection is going to be.

When asked in an interview whether he believed in God, Smith elaborated on his spiritual understanding:

I believe there are absolutely unquestionably forces at work in the universe that science can't explain. There is an end to human knowledge and beyond that into the unknown we have to call it something for us to be able to talk about it. . . . Let's agree there is something out there beyond our control; things happen in interesting ways that actually have patterns to them. There's things like karma, there are things that are mysteries. . . . I believe and try to tap in and understand and become a surfer of the Tao. To find that energy, whether it's energy, prayer. . . . So yes, I believe there is an energy and, yes, I try to connect to it and use it and be in the good graces of that energy to have things in my life go the way I like them to go.

In 2004, after meeting prominent Scientologist Tom Cruise during the filming of *Collateral*, the Smiths donated $20,000 to the Hollywood Education and Literacy Program (HELP), which serves as a foundation for Scientology's home-schooling. (Science-fiction author L. Ron Hubbard founded Scientology—the study of truth and the "handling of the spirit in relation to itself, others, and all of life.") In 2008, Smith and Pinkett Smith were criticized when they decided to fund New Village Leadership Academy, a private elementary school in Calabasas, California. The school employs teachers dedicated

From left, Wyclef Jean, Jada Pinkett Smith, Willow Smith, Will Smith, and Donna Summer watch Jaden Smith dance at the conclusion of the Nobel Peace Prize concert in Oslo, Norway, on December 11, 2009. Artists from all over the world gathered at the Oslo Spektrum to celebrate the year's Nobel Peace Prize laureate, President Barack Obama.

to Scientology and uses how-to-study methodologies, including Study Technology, developed by Hubbard. Jacqueline Olivier, an administrator at the academy, maintains that the school has no religious affiliations.

The Smiths, who are friends with Cruise and his wife, the actress Katie Holmes, have denied that they themselves are Scientologists. When asked directly about Scientology, Smith replied:

> As far as Scientology, I don't necessarily believe in organized religion. I was raised in a Baptist household, went to

a Catholic church, lived in a Jewish neighborhood, and had the biggest crush on the Muslim girls from one neighborhood over. Tom [Cruise] introduced me to the ideas.

CHARITY WORK

In recent years, the Smiths established the Will and Jada Smith Family Foundation in order to help benefit inner-city community development, youth educational projects, and underprivileged children and their families. The foundation is based in Maryland, where Pinkett Smith was born and raised. Her aunt, Karen Banfield Evans, is the executive director of the foundation. Evans notes, "Although we didn't necessarily consider ourselves 'philanthropists'—our family has always lived by the philosophy that you are your brother's keeper, and have done what we could to make our community better—whether that means helping family, neighbors, our church, or our community."

In 2006, the foundation donated $1 million to the high school from which Pinkett Smith graduated, the Baltimore School for the Arts. She requested that a theater at the school be established to help her honor Tupac Shakur's memory. Donald Hicken, Jada's former music teacher and head of the department since its founding in 1980, noted, "It means a lot when you're a teacher and your most famous alumnus comes back to give a donation. It really says a lot to the community that the school matters in people's lives."

In 2007, the Lupus Foundation of America (LFA) and Maybelline, in association with the Will and Jada Smith Family Foundation, hosted the first Butterflies Over Hollywood benefit in the El Rey Theatre in Los Angeles. More than 300 celebrities and guests helped to raise funds for the LFA. Jada Pinkett Smith was in attendance supporting her aunt, Karen Evans, who had almost died from complications of lupus. In 2008 alone, the Smiths donated more than $1.3 million to a variety of religious, civic, and arts groups through the Will and Jada Smith Family Foundation.

In January 2010, they announced that they are raising funds for the United Nations World Food Programme (WFP). These funds will be used to help feed the hungry in Haiti, who have lost so much since a 7.0 magnitude earthquake struck the island nation and devastated the capital of Port-au-Prince on January 12, 2010. Extensive damage to buildings will cost millions of dollars to repair. The number of dead is estimated to be more than 200,000. To raise money for Haitian relief, the Smiths have auctioned an artwork (to be sold on eBay) based on a map of world hunger and decorated with silhouettes drawn by Smith, his family, and the artists who performed at the Nobel Peace Prize concert that the Smiths cohosted in Oslo in December 2009. All those who contributed to its making also signed the artwork. By Smith's signature he wrote, "There can be no true peace in the world while there is hunger."

In addition, Smith took part in the "Hope for Haiti Now: A Global Benefit for Earthquake Relief" telethon that aired on January 22, 2010. Joel Gallen and Tenth Planet Productions produced the show, in collaboration with Viacom's MTV Networks and actor George Clooney. Other celebrities who took part in the telethon included Jennifer Aniston, Muhammad Ali, Drew Carey, Leonardo DiCaprio, Chris Rock, and Alyssa Milano. Performers included Coldplay, Mary J. Blige, Taylor Swift, and Jennifer Hudson. Mickelson Civil, a Haitian film-maker, also spoke at the event. He had to fight back tears as he talked about relatives who died and those who are barely surviving: "The survivors shouldn't have to go hungry or be afraid now." The telethon raised more than $60 million.

7

More Movie Madness

In December 2007, a catchy issue of *Entertainment Weekly* hit newsstands across the country. A close-up of Will Smith dominated the cover with the heading, "The 50 Smartest People in Hollywood" sprawled over Smith's forehead. He was listed at number 5, the highest-ranked actor after filmmakers Steven Spielberg and Judd Apatow. *Entertainment Weekly* declared, "[Will Smith] has revitalized and redefined old-fashion[ed] movie stardom in an era when movie stardom has become small and suspect ... achieving a level of global popularity unprecedented for an African-American actor."

I AM LEGEND

I Am Legend is a remake of the 1971 film *The Omega Man*, which had starred Charlton Heston as Robert Neville, the last man on Earth in the film. *The Omega Man* is itself a remake of a movie Vincent Price had starred in, *The Last Man on Earth* (1964). *I Am Legend*, based on the popular 1954 novel of the same name by Richard Matheson, was developed into a screenplay by Mark Protosevich and Akiva Goldsman.

I Am Legend appeared in theaters in 2007. Directed by Francis Lawrence, *I Am Legend* depicts a post-apocalyptic world in which Smith's character, Robert Neville, is a scientist trying to find a cure for a manufactured virus that has killed all humans except for a few of "the infected"—or man-eating zombies. In the first half of the movie, Smith appears almost always alone, with just his dog for company. When asked by an interviewer how it felt to play such a lonely character who begins to feel somewhat crazy, Smith responded:

> Basically, you are acting for the first half of the movie by yourself. It was such a wonderful exploration of myself. What happens is that you get in a situation where you don't have people to create the stimulus for you to respond to. What happens is that you start creating the stimulus and the response.

Smith believes he really had to stretch himself as an actor to pull off Neville's character. To ready himself for the film, he worked with Akiva Goldsman and the other writers. He also talked with a man who had been in isolation in prison to get a fuller idea of what it means to be alone. Smith had to lose a great deal of weight for the role, which for him is more difficult than putting on weight.

When filming the movie, the crew cleared six blocks surrounding Fifth Avenue in New York. When Smith walked down the center of the street with not a person in sight, he enjoyed the experience, but noted that was only because once the director yelled "cut," the streets would be filled with people once again. He told one interviewer, "Human connection and the groups we form, and being a part of something that moves and changes the world, is such a basic and human and simple idea. There was absolutely no pleasure for me at all in experiencing that amount of loneliness and solitude."

Also acting in the film was Smith's daughter, Willow. When Smith described working with Willow on *I Am Legend*, he said:

> You don't work with Willow, you work *for* Willow. We make our kids audition; we don't do the whole nepotism thing. She loves it. We were shooting the bridge sequence, it was probably 29 degrees, and we watched the temperature gauge go down to 1, then negative. Willow's cold and irritable, but she looks at me and she says, "Daddy, I don't care how low it goes, I'm going to finish." Wow. I was like, "That's good, baby. Daddy's leaving."

The movie was a worldwide hit. *I Am Legend* brought in more than $77 million in its opening weekend in the United States Film reviewer James Berardinelli said, "Will Smith pulls off this half-insane role perfectly." Another critic for the *Village Voice* remarked:

> Smith is simply dazzling here, and for all the undeniably impressive work the actor has done on his physique for this

IN HIS OWN WORDS...

Will Smith keeps a positive outlook on life. He believes that no problem need go unresolved:

> Give me a problem, I'll give you a solution. I just love living. That's a feeling you can't fake. I'm glad every single day. I think that even the camera can feel that I'm a happy man.

role, what's most appealing about him is his active intelligence—how he thinks his way through a role—and his
capacity for human weakness. Watch him, especially, in the
scene where he nurses his wounded canine companion, and
later, when he refuses to abandon his "post" to follow fellow
disease-free survivor Anna (*City of God* star Alice Braga) to
a supposed survivor's colony in (where else?) Vermont. If he
just stays put in his lab, he tells her, testing one vaccine after
another, he's sure he can put things right. There's a manic
edge to Neville by that point, and Smith makes you feel every
inch of his impotent rage. In what has been a pretty remark-
able career up to now, it's this performance that fully affirms
Smith as one of the great leading men of his generation.

HANCOCK

Smith's next film, *Hancock*, directed by Peter Berg and written by Vincent Ngo and Vince Gilligan, opened in theaters
in July 2008. Smith's Overbrook Entertainment produced the
film. Costarring in the film are Charlize Theron, Jason Bate-
man, and Jae Head. Smith plays the title character, Hancock,
a superhero crime fighter who hates his job and drinks too
much whiskey.

Berg enjoyed working with Smith on the film. Berg told
USA Today, "[Smith] has thought out every scene, every word
in the screenplay, and he has a theory about all of them. He's
scary smart. He plays chess. He taught us all how to solve the
Rubik's Cube (a skill he learned for *Happyness*), though he's
still the only guy who can do it."

At the film's premiere on July 2, 2008, Smith and his former
partner, DJ Jazzy Jeff, performed. On the same day *Hancock*
opened, Smith's daughter, Willow, had a movie premiere of
her own, for *Kit Kittredge: An American Girl*. Willow would
tell an interviewer, "[My dad] told me, 'Feel the moment.' He
is a really good actor. Sometimes he really feels the moment

and sometimes he doesn't and sometimes it just messes up the whole thing." Although those involved were happy with the film, *Hancock* was not well received by critics. The *San Francisco Chronicle* said of the film:

> Smith has become a good actor over the years. Ten years ago, he was a likable fellow with a knack for the wisecrack, but he's grown into something deeper, and Charlize Theron matches him in several heartfelt scenes. But either due to the overall subject matter or to some missed notes in Berg's

The Smith Kids: Trey, Jaden, and Willow

Following in the paths of their famous parents, the three Smith family children are already quite accomplished. All have budding careers in film or sport and actively participate in the family's extensive charity work and travels.

The oldest, Willard "Trey" Smith III, was born on November 11, 1992, in Los Angeles. He is the son of Will Smith and his first wife, Sheree Zampino. His stepmother, Jada Pinkett Smith, affectionately calls him her "bonus son." Trey attended a private school, Oaks Christian High School, located in Westlake Village, California, where he was wide receiver for his varsity football team. Two of his teammates were Nick Montana, son of former NFL star Joe Montana, and Trevor Gretzky, son of former NHL star Wayne Gretzky.

Young Trey was the inspiration for his father's pop song "Just the Two of Us," and he starred in its video production. He has also served as special correspondent for several Access Hollywood events, including Nickelodeon's Kids Choice Awards. Trey played a guest role in *All of Us*, the television series produced by his father and stepmother, and he also appeared at several promotional events for *The Pursuit of Happyness*, a film costarring his father and younger brother, Jaden. In recent years, Trey has shown interest in furthering his talents on the soccer field.

Jaden Christopher Syre Smith was born to Will and Jada on July 8, 1998, in Los Angeles, California. At the 2007 MTV Movie Awards, Jaden won the Best Breakthrough Performance award for his starring role as five-year-old Christopher in *The Pursuit of Happyness* (2006). He has also appeared in direction, the movie feels trivial as an emotional piece and never takes off as an action movie.

And *Time* called *Hancock* "strenuous, smartly made, and ordinary to an extraordinary degree."

Even with criticism being made about the film, Smith's undeniable ability to draw crowds and sell tickets remained: Fans simply like to watch Smith on the big screen. The film made over $62 million during its first weekend in the United States alone. James Berardinelli noted:

All of Us and the Disney Channel's *The Suite Life of Zach and Cody*. Jaden will star as Dre, a bullied youth—with Jackie Chan playing his eccentric martial arts mentor—in the June 2010 release of *The Karate Kid*, a remake of the 1980s classic.

The youngest Smith child, Willow Camille Reign Smith, was born to Will and Jada in Los Angeles on October 31, 2000. Willow made her acting debut alongside her father in *I Am Legend* (2007). Her next major film was *Kit Kittredge: An American Girl* (2008). Already mature and focused for her age, her parents describe Willow's personality and character as having the "independence" of her mother and the "work ethic" of her father.

Both Jaden and Willow are homeschooled, which allows them to travel with their parents, as needed, when shooting films on location. Jada noted, "We have tutors and a little schoolroom with other children . . . they love it." Jaden and Will also serve as youth ambassadors for Hasbro corporation's Project Zambi, which assists an estimated 15 million children orphaned by AIDS in Africa.

All three children are regularly involved in the work of the Will and Jada Smith Family Foundation. In an interview with *Child Magazine*, Jada explained, "That's part of what we do [as] a family: Giving back is a must. At least once every three months, the kids visit an orphanage or a homeless shelter or a nursing home and sit down with the families and children. My kids are very willing to give things away because they understand that they have such abundance; they don't have to hoard."

Young actress Willow Smith and her father, Will Smith, arrive at the premiere of her film *Kit Kittredge: An American Girl* at The Grove in Los Angeles, California, in 2008.

To the extent that *Hancock* works, it's largely because of Will Smith, whose performance is stronger than what this otherwise scattershot production deserves. *Hancock* is sometimes funny, sometimes clever, and occasionally involving, but it's never brilliant and its edge is compromised by the neutering that accompanies the teen-friendly PG-13 rating.

Rolling Stone noted, "As for Smith, he's on fire. There's nothing like a star shining on his highest beams. You follow him anywhere."

SEVEN POUNDS

In 2008, Smith produced and starred in the film *Seven Pounds*. In this movie, directed by Gabriele Muccino and written by Grant Nieporte, Smith's character, Ben, sets out to change the lives of seven people. Also starring in the film are Rosario Dawson, Woody Harrelson, and Connor Cruise (who is the son of Smith's good friend, Tom Cruise, and the actress Nicole Kidman). When asked what attracted him to this movie, Smith told his interviewer, "I was attracted to *Seven Pounds* because there were ideas. There were emotions. There were parts of this character that I was hiding myself from. . . . I took *Seven Pounds* almost as a self-examination—as a self-exploration."

Working with Muccino on the film, Smith again found himself stretched as an actor. He explained to one interviewer:

One of the major things that I connected to [in working on *Seven Pounds*] was the idea that death is not the end. . . . My character didn't realize that it wasn't just a cliff that you fall off and everything is over. Life goes on and new flowers will be born, the birds will come back and all of that, if you allow yourself to be open to it and accept the idea. This movie's almost a cautionary tale about that idea, because he realized it too late.

Shown from left, Will Smith, Rosario Dawson, and director Gabriele Muccino discuss a scene from their film *Seven Pounds* (2008). Over the years, Smith has gained considerable respect for being both a box-office star as well as a serious actor.

In order to express his character's intense pain and turmoil on film, Smith used the passing of his grandmother, who had died of a stroke a few years earlier, as inspiration. He said of her death, "I never cried about it and always adopted the attitude she was in a better place, that it was for the best because of the stroke and how ill she was. I'm sure I drew on that because it gave me permission to feel things that you don't normally or I don't normally like to show. I guess it's healing in that way."

Reviewers by and large did not like the film, calling it slow and sufferable for the audience. A few critics, however, including Roger Ebert, enjoyed it. He was especially smitten with Smith's performance:

> Will Smith displays a rather impressive range of emotional speeds here. He can be a tough, merciless IRS man. He can bend the rules on some cases. He can have a candlelight dinner with a beautiful woman named Emily Posa (Rosario Dawson) and go home afterward. She can sense his deep sadness. He is angry with people sometimes, but he seems angriest of all at himself. It's quite a performance.

In addition to producing this film, Smith has worked on several movies in which he did no acting, but served exclusively as producer. By way of his production company, Overbrook Entertainment, Smith helped to produce *Lakeview Terrace*, *The Human Contract*, and *The Secret Life of Bees* in 2008 and *The Karate Kid* in 2010.

8

What's Next for Will Smith?

As Smith noted in a *Reader's Digest* interview, his philosophy is simple: "I can do it." This can-do attitude has allowed him to focus his attention and achieve great things. His winning persona has shown the world that a black entertainer can appeal to all races and ages. His widespread appeal is a result of his approachable, disarming demeanor, his intelligence and wit,

IN HIS OWN WORDS...

Will Smith once described the differences between being an actor and a musician:

As an actor you're a tool for the director. As a musician you're exploring and displaying the essence of you.

Will Smith's Accolades

Throughout his career, Will Smith has received numerous accolades for his work as both an actor and a rapper. A sampling of his awards is listed below:

WON

2009 BET Awards, Favorite Actor

2008 Saturn Awards, Best Actor for *I Am Legend*

2002 BET Awards, Favorite Actor

2000 ASCAP Awards, Most Performed Songs for *Wild Wild West*

1999 Image Awards, Entertainer of the Year
ShoWest Awards, Actor of the Year
Blockbuster Awards, Favorite Actor for *Enemy of the State*

1998 Blockbuster Awards, Favorite Actor for *Men in Black*
ASCAP Awards, Most Performed Songs for *Men in Black*
MTV Movie Awards, Best Fight for *Men in Black*
MTV Movie Awards, Best Song for *Men in Black*

1997 Grammy Awards, Best Rap Solo Performance for *Men in Black*
MTV Movie Awards, Best Kiss for *Independence Day*
Blockbuster Awards, Favorite Actor for *Independence Day*
ShoWest Convention, International Box Office Achievement

1995 ShoWest Convention, Male Star of Tomorrow

1991 Grammy Awards, Best Rap Duo Performance for "Summertime"

1988 Grammy Awards, Best Rap Performance for "Parents Just Don't Understand"

NOMINATED

2007 Academy Awards, Best Actor for *The Pursuit of Happyness*

2002 Academy Awards, Best Actor for *Ali*
Golden Globe Awards, Best Actor for *Ali*

2000 Blockbuster Awards, Favorite Action Team for *Wild Wild West*
Blockbuster Awards, Favorite Song for *Wild Wild West*

(continues)

(continued)

1999   Image Awards, Outstanding Lead Actor for *Enemy of the State*
MTV Movie Awards, Best Performance for *Enemy of the State*

1998   MTV Movie Awards, Best Comedic Performance for *Men in Black*
MTV Movie Awards, Best On-Screen Duo for *Men in Black*

1997   Image Awards, Outstanding Lead Actor for *Fresh Prince of Bel-Air*
MTV Movie Awards, Best Performance for *Independence Day*

1996   Image Awards, Outstanding Lead Actor for *Fresh Prince of Bel-Air*
MTV Movie Awards, Best On-Screen Duo for *Bad Boys*

1994   Golden Globe Awards, Best Actor for *Fresh Prince of Bel-Air*

1993   Golden Globe Awards, Best Actor for *Fresh Prince of Bel-Air*

his positive outlook on life, his strategic selection of content and format based on an in-depth analysis of what sells, and his undeniable, brilliantly inspired on-screen talent. He has already created a legacy that is bound to grow and exert an even bigger influence as Smith moves into the next stage of his life and his career. He said in one interview, "My goal is to be the most diverse actor in the history of Hollywood. When I look back, I don't want there to be one person who has a more colorful spectrum of films."

THE FUTURE

Smith continues to keep his hands in many projects and shows no signs of slowing down. Actor, musician, producer, investor, writer, philanthropist—he is certainly not afraid to try new ventures. In addition to acting, he is especially interested in the running of his production company, Overbrook Entertainment, and uses it to produce the diversified, high-quality

Will Smith poses with family and friends during a hand and footprint ceremony honoring him at Grauman's Chinese Theatre in Hollywood, California, on December 10, 2007. Fellow actor and good friend Tom Cruise stands at far right.

music, television, and films that he believes in. Currently, he has a large number of films in development, including an *I Am Legend* prequel, *Men in Black III, Hancock 2,* and *I, Robot 2,* among others.

Even if he were to never make another film, Will Smith has already left a considerable mark on the entertainment world. In 2004, 2005, and 2006, he was named one of the 50 Most Powerful People in Hollywood. In 2005, *Premiere* ranked him at number 44 on a list of the Greatest Movie Stars of All Time for its "Stars in Our Constellation" feature. In 2006, *Time* named Smith one of the 100 Most Influential People. In

2007, *Entertainment Weekly* named Smith one of the Top 25 Entertainers of the Year. In 2007 and 2008, Forbes.com named Smith one of the 100 Most Powerful Celebrities. And his popularity has reaped considerable financial rewards: In 2004, his net worth was estimated to be $188 million; in 2007, *Forbes* estimated his earnings for the year at $31 million.

Will Smith is definitely one of the elite few who have made it from star to superstar. So where will Smith's next move take him?

Smith has joked with interviewers more than once that one day he might run for president: "People laugh, but if I set my mind to it, within the next 15 years I would be president." Or is he joking? With Will Smith, nothing appears to be impossible.

Selected Works

TELEVISION

1990–1996   *The Fresh Prince of Bel-Air*

FILM

1993   *Six Degrees of Separation*

1995   *Bad Boys*

1996   *Independence Day*

1997   *Men in Black*

1998   *Enemy of the State*

1999   *Wild Wild West*

2000   *The Legend of Bagger Vance*

2001   *Ali*

2002   *Men in Black II*

2003   *Bad Boys II*

2004   *I, Robot*; *Shark Tale*

2005   *Hitch*

2006   *The Pursuit of Happyness*

2007   *I Am Legend*

2008   *Hancock*; *Seven Pounds*

2011   *Men in Black III*

AS PRODUCER

1994–1996   *The Fresh Prince of Bel-Air* (executive producer)

2002   *Showtime* (executive producer)

2003   *Ride or Die* (executive producer); *All of Us* (executive producer, 2003–2007)

2004   *I, Robot* (executive producer); *The Seat Filler* (executive producer); *Saving Face* (producer)

2005   *Hitch* (producer)

2006   *The Pursuit of Happyness* (producer)

2008   *Hancock* (producer); *The Secret Life of Bees* (producer);
The Human Contract (executive producer); *Lakeview
Terrace* (producer); *Seven Pounds* (producer)

2010   *The Karate Kid* (producer)

Chronology

1968   Willard Christopher Smith Jr. is born on September 25 in West Philadelphia, Pennsylvania.

1986   Smith and Jeff Townes performed in Battle of the Bands at the New Music Seminar as DJ Jazzy Jeff and the Fresh Prince.

1987   Smith and Townes release their debut album, *Rock the House*, making Smith a millionaire; Smith graduates from high school.

1990   Smith stars in NBC's *The Fresh Prince of Bel-Air*, a sitcom that runs for six seasons.

1992   Smith debuts in his first movie role in *Where the Day Takes You*; marries Sheree Zampino; his first son, Willard "Trey" Smith III, is born.

1993   Smith hosts the Presidential Inaugural Celebration for Youth, part of the Gala for President Bill Clinton.

1995   Smith and Zampino divorce.

1996   Smith stars in the blockbuster movie *Independence Day*.

1997   Smith marries Jada Pinkett; stars in the blockbuster *Men in Black*.

1998   Smith's pop song "Just the Two of Us" is released; his second son, Jaden Christopher Syre Smith, is born.

2000   Smith's daughter, Willow Camille Reign Smith, is born.

2001   Smith's children's book, *Just the Two of Us*, is published; Smith takes part in "A Tribute to Heroes," the telethon for victims of the 9/11 bombings; he is a best-actor Oscar nominee for the film *Ali*.

2003   Smith and Pinkett Smith produce UPN's sitcom *All of Us*.

2004   Smith stars in the blockbuster movie *I, Robot*.

2006   Smith and son Jaden costar in *The Pursuit of Happyness*, for which Smith is nominated for an Academy Award.

2007   Smith stars in the internationally acclaimed blockbuster film *I Am Legend*.

2009 Smith and Pinkett Smith host a concert in Oslo, Norway, honoring the year's Nobel Peace Prize winner, President Barack Obama.

2010 Smith produced a remake of *The Karate Kid*, which stars Jackie Chan and his son, Jaden.

Miles, Liz. *Will Smith.* Chicago: Raintree, 2010.

Smith, Will. *Just the Two of Us.* New York: Scholastic Press, 2001.

Mitchell, Susan K. *Today's Superstars Entertainment: Will Smith.* Milwaukee, Wisc.: Gareth Stevens, 2007.

WEB SITES

All Music Guide, Will Smith
http://allmusic.com/cg/amg.dll?p=amg&sql=11:gbfpxquhld0e

The Internet Movie Database, Will Smith
http://www.imdb.com/name/nm0000226/

Overbrook Entertainment
http://www.overbrookent.com/

Will and Jada Smith Family Foundation
http://www.looktothestars.org/charity/68-will-and-jada-smith-family-foundation

Will Smith's Facebook page
http://www.facebook.com/WillSmith

Picture Credits

page

3: BEN STANSALL/AFP/Getty Images

9: ScottGries/Getty Images Entertainment/Getty Images

13: Ebet Roberts/Redferns/Getty Images

21: AP Images

23: © Neal Preston/CORBIS

32: 20th Century Fox/Photofest

42: Peter Brandt/Getty Images Entertainment/Getty Images

50: TOBY MELVILLE/Reuters/ Landov

53: © Photos 12/Alamy

59: Jason Merritt/FilMagic/Getty Images

67: John McConnico/AP Images

76: Todd Williamson/WireImage/ Getty Images

78: © Columbia Pictures

83: Nick Ut/AP Images

Anne M. Todd has a Bachelor of Arts degree in English and American Indian studies from the University of Minnesota. She has written more than 20 nonfiction children's books. They include biographies of world political leaders, entertainers, and American Indians, as well as several accounts of notable events in American history. Todd is also the author of the following Chelsea House books: *Roger Maris, Chris Rock, Jamie Foxx, Tyra Banks, Susan B. Anthony, Venus and Serena Williams,* and *Vera Wang.* Todd lives in Prior Lake, Minnesota, with her husband, Sean, and three sons, Spencer, William, and Henry.